History Around You

Nick Hunter

raintree
a Capstone company — publishers for children

Raintree is an imprint of Capstone Global Library Limited, a company incorporated in England and Wales having its registered office at 7 Pilgrim Street, London, EC4V 6LB – Registered company number: 6695582

www.raintreepublishers.co.uk
myorders@raintreepublishers.co.uk

Text © Capstone Global Library Limited 2015
First published in hardback in 2014
First published in paperback in 2015
The moral rights of the proprietor have been asserted.

Edited by Catherine Veitch and Gina Kammer
Designed by Steve Mead and Peggie Carley
Picture research by Mica Brancic
Production by Helen McCreath
Originated by Capstone Global Library Ltd
Printed and bound in China by RR Donnelley Asia

ISBN 978 1 406 28150 7 (hardback))

18 17 16 15 14
10 9 8 7 6 5 4 3 2 1

ISBN 978 1 406 28154 5 (paperback)

19 18 17 16 15
10 9 8 7 6 5 4 3 2 1

British Library Cataloguing in Publication Data
A full catalogue record for this book is available from the British Library.

Acknowledgements
We would like to thank the following for permission to reproduce photographs:

Alamy: John Smith, 24, National Geographic Image Collection, 5, Scottish Viewpoint, 19; Getty Images: cover, Hulton Archive, 6, Hulton Archive/Central Press, 20, Lonely Planet Images/Neil Setchfield, 14, Photolibrary/Spencer Grant, 7, Picture Post/ Haywood Magee, 22; iStock: cvoogt, 11, mashabuba, 9; Shutterstock: Antonio Abrignani, 28, Elwood Chu, 4, I. Pilon, 18, Jane Rix, 26, Jorge Salcedo, 10, Kiev.Victor, 15, Tupungato, 13; SuperStock: age fotostock/Richard Levine, 23, age fotostock/Walter Bibikow, 12, The Art Archive, 16, ClassicStock.com, 8, 17, imagebroker.net, 25, Robert Harding Picture Library, 27, Science and Society, 21, UpperCut Images, 29

Every effort has been made to contact copyright holders of material reproduced in this book. Any omissions will be rectified in subsequent printings if notice is given to the publisher.

Contents

Some words are shown in bold, **like this**.
You can find out what they mean by looking
in the glossary.

History and you

When we learn about history, we discover how people lived in the past. We can find out about people who lived hundreds of years ago in faraway parts of the world.

▲ These warrior statues were made more than 2,000 years ago in China.

There is also lots of history in the place where you live. You can find history all around you, in the smallest town or in a busy city. You can find history in your local area in many ways.

Many towns are a mixture of old and modern buildings. Can you spot the old building here?

Changing times

Look around on your way to school and you will see your neighbourhood changing. Look out for new homes being built. You may see a new playground opening or shops closing down.

▲ This is a busy San Francisco street more than 100 years ago.

Over many years, these everyday changes will make your neighbourhood very different. The pictures on these pages show how a town has changed over 100 years.

▲ Today the same busy street looks very different.

Asking questions

If you want to find out about local history, start asking some questions. Your parents and grandparents can tell you how the area has changed since they were at school.

▲ Ask your teachers how your school has changed.

You can use historical sources to find out about local history. **Primary sources** are things that have survived from the time. **Secondary sources** include books or films that were made later.

▲ Old photos are primary sources. They show what people and places looked like in the past.

Homes

Do you live in a new or old home? You may find your house on old photos or maps. If the homes nearby look the same, they were probably all built around the same time.

▲ The buildings in this neighbourhood were built more than 100 years ago.

Try to find the oldest homes in your area. Hundreds of years ago, homes were built of wood or stone rather than bricks. Older brick houses were often built for rich people.

▲ Some old wooden houses have been changed or added onto by families that live in them today.

Public buildings

Many old houses built of wood have been replaced with newer homes. Many public buildings were built of stone so they are still standing. These buildings include town halls or meeting places. You can still visit them today.

▲ This courthouse was built in 1907.

Churches are often the oldest buildings in a town. Local people have been visiting this stone church for hundreds of years. Churches contain records of local people who were members there.

▲ When it was first built, this church would have been taller than the buildings around it.

Remembering people

In churchyards and **cemeteries** you can find the graves of people who lived in the local area. Gravestones show the date people were born and when they died. Richer people built large tombs.

▲ These grand tombs are in Glasgow, Scotland.

Sometimes **monuments** and statues were built to remember people. The names of people who died in a war are often listed on war memorials.

▲ You can find war memorials in many towns and villages.

Pictures and photographs

Pictures will show you what life was like. Before photographs were invented, artists would paint **portraits** of rich families. Most ordinary people could not afford to pay for portraits.

▲ This picture was painted in 1853. What can it tell us about children's lives at that time?

Old photographs tell us a lot about how people lived. One hundred years ago, photographers took family portraits. The families wore their best clothes. Photos were only in black and white.

▲ Family photos in the past were more serious than photos we take now.

Local museums

Many places have a local museum. In a big city, a museum can be very large. In a small town, a museum could be in a single room. Museum displays include pictures and objects from the past.

▲ Museums collect ancient objects, such as this stone arrowhead.

The museum may keep old records from your town. Before telephones and the **Internet** were invented, people wrote letters to friends and family. Letters can tell us what people did in their everyday lives.

▲ In the past, important documents were written out by hand and stored in libraries.

Reading the news

Many years ago, newspapers were the only way to find out what was happening in the local area and around the world. Old newspapers will tell you what happened on any day in the past.

▲ These people are buying newspapers to tell them about the first man to travel into space.

Old posters and **advertisements** can also tell us a lot about how people lived in the past. Advertisements were eye-catching or colourful to make people buy things.

This poster is advertising seaside holidays.

CONEY BEACH
PORTHCAWL

WATER-CHUTE

OUTINGS
to Britain's Brightest Pleasure Beach

WRITE MANAGER, CONEY BEACH, PORTHCAWL
FOR ILLUSTRATED BOOKLETS AND MENUS   BRITISH RAILWAYS

Changing communities

Your town may be home to the children or grandchildren of people who moved from other countries. Your own family may once have lived somewhere very different.

▲ Many **immigrants** moved to the United Kingdom from the Caribbean during the 1950s.

Find out why immigrants from other countries moved to your area. Ask older people what they found difficult when they first arrived. How have things changed since they have lived in your area?

▲ Immigrants often bring colourful festivals and music to their new home countries.

Work and play

Many jobs that people did in the past are less common today. Factories have closed down. Some factories may have changed into homes or apartments.

▲ This old factory and canal were once used to make and transport goods.

Many sports teams have been part of a local area for many years. When were your local teams started? Your teams may have old photos to help you explore their history.

▲ Compare old photos and modern photos to see how local sports teams have changed.

Famous events and people

A major historical event could have happened in your area in the past. Look out for special museums or monuments. They may be there to remember a battle or a famous person from your town.

▲ This museum was built to look like the original home of the famous writer William Shakespeare.

Many museums are close to important historic sites. **Archaeologists** dig beneath the ground to find out about people who lived hundreds of years ago.

▲ Many historical clues are hidden under the ground.

Your local history project

Find out as much as you can about your local area. Try to find primary sources from your area's past. You can also ask adults for help to **interview** people who have lived in your town for many years.

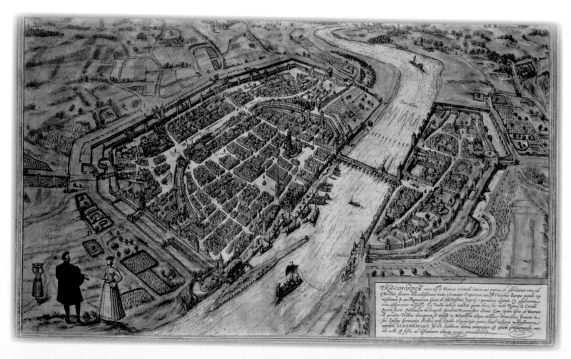

▲ Comparing old and new maps will show how your city has changed. This map was made in 1572.

Collect everything you find out about your area in a scrapbook. If you can collect photos and other information on a computer, it will be easier to share your project with your family and friends.

▲ You could ask your parent or teacher to help you put together a **website** to share what you have learned.

Find out more

Books

A City Through Time, Steve Noon (Dorling Kindersley, 2013)

Your Local History (Unlocking History), Brian Williams (Heinemann Library, 2010)

Websites

www.bbc.co.uk/history/handsonhistory/local-history.shtml
See a video guide to researching local history.

www.nationalarchives.gov.uk/victorians/Default.aspx
Click on "Local History" to find out how to investigate what your area was like in Victorian times.

Glossary

advertisement information, such as on a poster or on TV, that tries to make people buy something

archaeologist someone who digs in the ground to uncover remains from the past

cemetery area in many towns and cities where people are buried when they die

immigrant someone who moves to a new country from the country where they were born

Internet system of connected computers that we can use to send and receive information around the world

interview conversation in which one person is being asked lots of questions to get information

monument statue or other object that was put up to remember an event or person

portrait painting or photograph of a person or group of people

primary source object, document, picture, or recording that dates from the time being studied

secondary source source, such as a book, that describes a time but was written or created later

website collection of words, pictures, and other features that can be accessed with a computer via the Internet

Index

Fast

Fabric Gifts

scrap fabric style • small scale sewing • thrifty chic

Sally Southern

David and Charles

For Kitty

A DAVID & CHARLES BOOK
Copyright © David & Charles Limited 2010

David & Charles is an imprint of F&W Media International, Ltd
Brunel House, Forde Close, Newton Abbot, TQ12 4PU, UK

F&W Media International, Ltd is a subsidiary of F+W Media,Inc
10151 Carver Road, Suite #200, Blue Ash , OH 45242, USA

First published in the UK in 2010
Reprinted in 2011

Text and designs copyright © Sally Southern 2010
Layout and photography copyright © David & Charles 2010

A catalogue record for this book is available from the British Library.

ISBN-13: 978-0-7153-3040-1 paperback
ISBN-10: 0-7153-3040-3 paperback

Printed in China by RR Donnelley
for David & Charles
Brunel House   Newton Abbot   Devon

Commissioning Editor: Jennifer Fox-Proverbs
Editor: Bethany Dymond
Art Editors: Charly Bailey and Sarah Clark
Cover Design: Victoria Marks
Project Editor: Cathy Joseph
Production Controller: Bev Richardson
Photographer: Ginette Chapman

F&W Media International, LTD publishes high quality books on a wide range
of subjects. For more great book ideas visit: www.stitchcraftcreate.co.uk

Contents

Just for the home

Sew pretty...

Everyone loves pretty little gifts, especially if they are hand crafted and unique. Here, you can discover how to create many fantastic pieces for your friends, your family and, most importantly, for yourself!

Using your favourite fabrics, trimmings and embellishments, you can make all manner of keepsakes, from jewellery and picture frames to bead jars and bags. The projects are all simple to make and suitable for even the most inexperienced of crafters, with the emphasis as much on the fabulous fabrics used as the techniques.

The equipment needed is basic and inexpensive – mainly just a simple sewing kit – and you will find all that you need to get started for each project in the materials lists. The fabrics you use need not be expensive either. Many of the projects require only a small amount of material, so you can choose anything from the most sumptuous silks to sweet cotton florals, from funky contemporary prints to vintage fabrics. You can even recycle old clothing for a more personal feel. Combine these with a selection of buttons, beads, ribbons and trimmings for truly stunning results!

Matching the fabrics to suit your taste or to coordinate with your home is what makes every project truly unique and the designs in this book can easily be adapted to fit in with your personal preferences. Simply use them as a starting point to take your creativity further and make something even more special.

Hopefully, this book will inspire you to make the projects in several different fabrics and colour schemes to have fun creating something really exceptional and achieve a different look each time. **Happy stitching!**

Just for you

Keeping a note

Make your notebook, sketchbook or diary extra special and personal by covering it with pretty fabrics and appliquéd birds. It will guarantee to turn your book into a precious keepsake for years to come. A photo album, covered in the same way, will make a delightful collection of treasured memories. You can use the leftover fabrics to make a pretty pencil case to match (see page 16).

Small wonder

The button eyes and wing flaps add gorgeous texture to the appliquéd birds

Materials

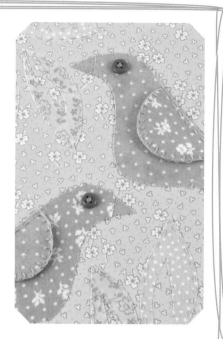

- ❖ Hardback notebook, A5 size – 15.5 x 22cm (6 x 8½in) approx.

- ❖ Fabrics:
  - ❖ yellow gingham 25 x 26cm (10 x 10½in)
  - ❖ yellow floral 18 x 26cm (7 x 10½in)
  - ❖ scraps in floral and spotted fabric, blue and green

- ❖ Embroidery threads – pale green, pale blue, peach (split the threads into three strands)

- ❖ Tiny blue buttons x 2

- ❖ Basic kit (see page 111)

Finished size

15.5 x 22cm (6 x 8½in)

LITTLE TIP

STICK TO A SIMPLE COLOUR SCHEME BASED ON TWO MAIN COLOURS TO GIVE THE DESIGN GREATER CONTRAST.

1 Pin the two pieces of yellow fabric right sides together along the 26cm (10½in) edge.

2 Open the seam and press flat with an iron.

3 Use the templates on page 120 to trace two birds, two beaks, two wings and five leaves on to Bondaweb. Roughly cut out and iron on to the back of the scraps of floral and spotted fabrics, then cut out the shapes carefully.

4 Take a wing shape and peel off the paper backing. Iron it on to the back of a contrasting fabric, then cut it out approximately 3mm (⅛in) from the edge of the shape. Repeat with the other wing, then put these to one side.

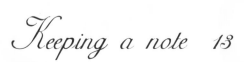

5 Peel the paper backing from the rest of the shapes and position on to the yellow fabric, overlapping slightly on to the gingham. When you're satisfied with the layout and have checked that the positioning will fit on to the front of the book, iron the shapes to fix in place.

6 Sew single stitches along the join of the yellow gingham and floral fabrics with pale green embroidery thread.

LITTLE TIP

WHEN ARRANGING YOUR LAYOUT, DRAW AROUND THE BOOK ON TO THE BACKGROUND FABRIC USING VANISHING PEN SO THAT YOU KNOW WHERE TO PLACE THE PIECES.

7 Use the blue thread to sew tiny catch stitches around the birds to secure in place. Use peach thread to sew the wings in place with running stitch, then continue around the edge of the wing using a blanket stitch, so that the wing is only joined to the bird along the top edge. Sew running stitch around the edge of the leaves and stitch the small blue buttons in place for the bird's eyes.

8 Stick the fabric on to the cover of the book with double-sided tape, folding over the edges and sticking them inside the book cover. Hide all the raw edges inside the book by sticking the front and back pages over them.

Pretty pencil case

Keep all your pens and pencils zipped up together with this delightful matching case. Printing the fabrics on to paper and covering a handful of pencils enhances the sweetness of the look.

1 Using the template on page 120, cut out two panels, the front in floral fabric and the back in gingham, backing the fabric with iron-on stabiliser first if the fabrics are very thin.

2 Trace the bird shapes on to Bondaweb and then iron on to the back of the fabric scraps. Make the wing as for the notebook (page 13). Position bird pieces on to the floral fabric, peel off backing paper and iron in place. Stitch around the outside to secure (pages 14–15). Sew on the button for the eye and use a vanishing pen to draw swirls by the beak. Sew along these lines with running stitch, then weave the same coloured thread through the stitches to make a solid line.

3 Fold and press the top edges of the front and back panels under by 1cm (⅜in). Pin both pieces along the zip and machine stitch. Fold the pencil case inside out and pin around the edges. Machine stitch, then snip the bottom corners diagonally and turn through to the right side. Press flat. Finish by looping the thin gingham ribbon through the zip pull.

Materials

- ❖ Fabrics:
  - ❖ yellow gingham 12 x 28cm (4¾ x 11in)
  - ❖ yellow floral 12 x 28cm (4¾ x 11in)
  - ❖ scraps of blue and green
- ❖ Iron-on stabiliser backing
- ❖ Yellow zip 20cm (8in)
- ❖ Tiny blue button
- ❖ Embroidery threads – pale green, blue, peach (split into three strands)
- ❖ Thin blue gingham ribbon 16cm (6¼in)
- ❖ Pencils
- ❖ Paper with colour-copied fabric
- ❖ Basic kit (see page 111)

Finished size
10 x 26cm (4 x 10½in)

LITTLE TIP
COPY YOUR FABRICS ON TO PAPER WITH A PHOTOCOPIER AND WRAP AROUND PENCILS, SECURING WITH DOUBLE-SIDED TAPE.

Funky floral jewellery set

Statement jewellery has never been more popular and these pieces will certainly turn heads! Using ready-made felt beads and a hand-sewn flower to make a quirky bracelet is so easy and you can jazz it up as much as you like by adding all your favourite seed beads and sequins too. You can rustle up the funky ring on page 23 in no time at all and the necklace on page 24 will complete the stylish set.

Small wonder

Decorate each felt bead with your seed beads and sequins in a slightly different way for a random, quirky look

Materials

- ❖ Felt beads – pinks and purples
- ❖ Felt – burgundy, deep pink
- ❖ Iridescent sequins
- ❖ Embroidery thread – pale pink, mid pink
- ❖ Strong thread
- ❖ Findings – bracelet fastening
- ❖ Basic kit (see page 111)

Finished size
23cm (9in) approx.

LITTLE TIP

NEPAL WOOL FELT IS OFTEN
THICKER THAN REGULAR
FELT AND WILL MAKE YOUR
FLOWERS STURDIER.

1 Before you start, place the felt beads in a line to find out which layout works best. Quickly join them together with a needle and thread to check that they will fit around your wrist, then separate them again.

2 Decorate the felt beads by stitching on small seed beads and sequins. To do this, make a small knot in some strong thread and pull through a felt bead using a beading needle. Slip a bead on to the needle and then push back through to the opposite side of the bead. Repeat until you have covered the felt bead evenly with seed beads. You can also stitch sequins with seed beads in the centre on to the felt beads.

3 Using embroidery thread split into three strands, thread the felt beads together, adding two iridescent sequins between each one. Once threaded together, stitch a small jump ring to one end and a clasp to the other to fasten the bracelet.

4 Use the templates on page 119 to cut a large flower out of felt and then a smaller flower out of lighter coloured felt in a similar tone.

5 Split matching embroidery thread into three strands and, with a single strand, sew tiny running stitches around the edge of each flower.

6 Place the smaller flower on top of the larger one and sew together with a small felt bead with a sequin and seed bead at the centre. Sew the corsage flower on to one of the small felt beads on the bracelet.

LITTLE TIP

TEST THE LENGTH OF THE BRACELET AROUND YOUR WRIST BEFORE YOU ADD THE CLASP AND JUMP RING IN CASE IT NEEDS ADJUSTING.

Ring the changes

Diamonds may be a girl's best friend but this eyecatching felt ring really has the wow factor and it can be made up in a trice using the same corsage flower technique as the bracelet.

Materials

- Felt bead – lime green
- Felt – jade, turquoise
- Seed beads
- Embroidery thread
  – pale turquoise, mid blue
- Findings – ring base
- Strong glue
- Basic kit (see page 111)

Finished size
3.5 x 3.5cm ($1^3/_8$ x $1^3/_8$in) approx.

1 Use the templates on page 119 to cut a large flower out of felt and then a smaller flower out of lighter coloured felt to make the outer and inner petals. Split matching embroidery thread into three strands and, with a single strand, sew tiny running stitches around the edge of each flower.

2 Place the smaller flower on top of the larger one and sew together with a small felt bead at the centre. Decorate the felt bead with extra seed beads. Use strong glue to stick the finished flower on to a ring base.

Fabulous in felt

Coordinate your bracelet and ring with a matching necklace, or use different colours to complement your favourite outfit. Positioning the flower off-centre looks more sophisticated.

Materials

❖ Felt beads – blues and greens

❖ Felt – jade, turquoise, lime

❖ Iridescent sequins

❖ Embroidery thread – pale turquoise, mid blue

❖ Selection of mid-sized glass beads – blues and greens

❖ Strong thread

❖ Findings – necklace fastening

❖ Basic kit (see page 111)

Finished size
70cm (28in) approx.

LITTLE TIP

THE EMBROIDERY THREAD NEEDS TO BE ABOUT THREE TIMES THE FINISHED LENTH OF THE NECKLACE. MAKE SURE IT'S LONG ENOUGH BEFORE YOU KNOT THE BEADS.

1 Select the felt beads you want to use and lay them in order. Make a flower in the same way as described for the bracelet (pages 21–22) and position it where you want amongst the felt beads. Space out all of the beads and add a smaller glass bead in between each felt bead. Decorate some felt beads with seed beads or sequins, leaving others plain.

2 Thread the beads together using embroidery thread. Space out the beads by tying knots in the thread above and below each bead to keep it in place. Stitch the corsage flower on to the embroidery thread to hold in place. Finish by stitching a jump ring and clasp on to each end of the necklace to fasten.

Out of the button box

Making your own covered buttons allows you to create personalized and coordinated embellishments, but they also make irresistible little keepsakes. Mounted on luggage labels covered with gorgeous papers, they can be mixed and matched with your cherished button box favourites. They are so versatile, you can also use them as the starting point for pretty little gifts, such as the cute corsage brooch on page 32.

Small wonder
Finish the buttons simply, or lavish each one with beads and embroidery

Materials

- ❖ Fabrics:
  - ❖ blue tweed scraps
  - ❖ blue silky floral print scraps

- ❖ 6 x ready to cover button blanks, 22mm (¾in) diameter

- ❖ Embroidery threads – navy, lime, turquoise

- ❖ Selection of seed beads and sequins

- ❖ Luggage label tags

- ❖ Printed paper (to complement fabrics)

- ❖ Thin wire

- ❖ Basic kit (see page 111)

Finished size
12 x 6cm (4¾ x 2⅜in) approx.

1 Cut out circles of fabrics larger than the button blanks (a guide to the size you need to cut should come with the button blanks). You will need six circles – three in tweed and three in the silky fabric.

2 Decorate each circle by adding beads, sequins or stitching to the centre. For example, you could sew a sequin with a bead in the middle on each of the floral print circles. For the tweed circles, sew either a flower made up of five individual chain stitches as petals with a bead in the middle, or a star with a bead at each point and a cluster of beads in the centre.

3 Once the circles have been decorated, place the fabric over the button blank, fold under the edges and snap the back on, ensuring that the beads/stitches are in the middle of the button.

LITTLE TIP

IF YOUR SILKY FABRIC IS HEAVILY
PATTERNED, YOU MAY NOT NEED TO
ADD STITCHING OR BEADING AS IT
WILL CONTRAST NICELY WITH THE
ROUGHER TEXTURE OF TWEED.

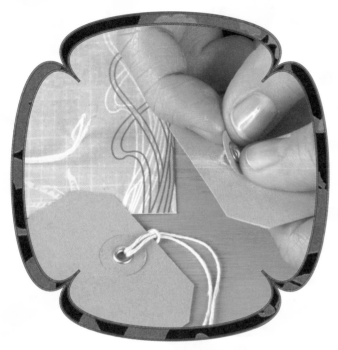

4 Take a luggage label tag and remove the string. Carefully remove the re-enforcement ring from the front of the label and put to one side.

LITTLE TIP

USE A CRAFT KNIFE TO CUT OUT
THE PAPER AS IT WILL GIVE A MUCH
CLEANER CUT THAN SCISSORS.

5 Stick the luggage label on to printed craft paper and use a craft knife, ruler and cutting mat to carefully cut it out so that the paper covers the front of the label.

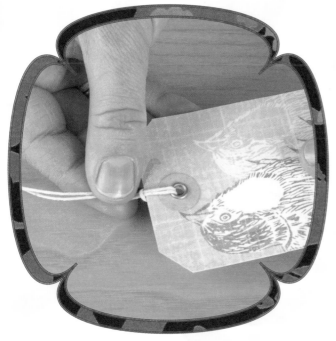

6 Make a hole at the top of the label and glue the re-enforcement ring back in position. Thread the string back on to the label.

7 On the back of the label mark the position for the six buttons and make holes. Fasten the buttons on to the label using either thin wire threaded through, or stitch them in place with embroidery thread.

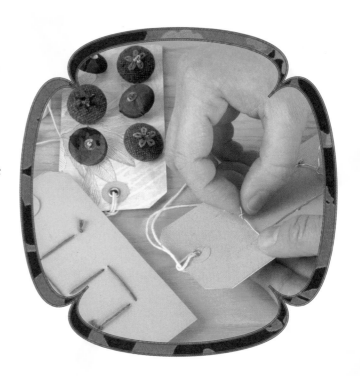

Out of the button box 31

Pin-up model

A covered button makes a perfect centrepiece for an attractive brooch. You could make the brooch larger and attach to a handbag, or stitch it to a luggage label, embellished with buttons.

LITTLE TIP

FUSING THE FABRICS TOGETHER WITH BONDAWEB BEFORE CUTTING OUT THE FLOWER SHAPES PREVENTS THE RAW EDGES FROM FRAYING.

1 Use Bondaweb to fuse two pieces of the silky fabric together, then use the template on page 119 to cut out a large flower shape. Fuse a piece of tweed fabric with the silky fabric and cut out a smaller flower using the template.

2 Sew tiny running stitches around the edge of the large flower in single strand turquoise embroidery thread. Stitch seed beads on to each petal of the tweed flower.

3 Place the small flower on top of the larger flower and stitch the covered button in the centre so that it holds all the pieces together. Sew the brooch pin on to the back.

4 If you wish, you can mount the corsage on to a covered luggage label (see pages 30–31) by stitching in place. Finish by sewing three small uncovered buttons at the bottom of the label.

Materials

❖ Fabrics:
   ❖ blue tweed scraps
   ❖ blue silky floral scraps

❖ Covered button (see pages 28–29)

❖ Seed beads

❖ Embroidery thread – turquoise

❖ Bought buttons – three complementary colours

❖ Brooch pin

❖ Covered label (see pages 30–31)

❖ Basic kit (see page 111)

Finished size
6 x 5.5cm (2½ x 2¼in) approx.

Cute cosmetic case

Use contrasting printed fabrics and ginghams for a super cute and feminine bag, just big enough to keep all your make-up bits 'n' bobs in one place. The fabric is combined with a clever touch of vintage-style floral with a smattering of seed beads for that extra pretty touch. The coordinating drawstring bags (see page 40) are just the thing you need to store all your essential toiletries – guaranteed to brighten up any bathroom.

Small wonder

Adding small beads and sequins to the floral panel on the front of the bag adds that little extra sparkle

Materials

- ❖ Fabrics:
  - ❖ blue star, 20 x 28cm (8 x 11in)
  - ❖ red gingham, 23 x 32cm (9 x 12½in) plus two pieces 13 x 6cm (5 x 2½in), plus another scrap
  - ❖ floral scrap
- ❖ Iron-on stabiliser
- ❖ Seed beads – red, clear
- ❖ Sequins – red
- ❖ Embroidery thread – red, green
- ❖ Large red button
- ❖ Thin red ribbon 10cm (4in) approx.
- ❖ Basic kit (see page 111)

Finished size
12 x 18cm (4¾ x 7in)

1 Back a scrap of floral fabric with Bondaweb and cut out around a sprig of flowers. Iron this piece on to a scrap of red gingham. Sew around the edge of the floral piece with red embroidery thread split into two strands, using running stitch. Add seed beads and red sequins to highlight certain parts of the flowers. Use a single strand of green thread to sew a stitch along the centre of each of the leaves. Cut the gingham so that it follows the shape of floral panel with a little room to spare, then fray the edges.

2 If the blue star fabric is thin then use iron-on stabiliser to add strength. Mark the base of the make-up bag, which is 12cm (4¾in) from each edge (the base is 4cm (1½in) wide). Stitch the floral piece so that it is in the middle of the top section of the star fabric. Pin the 13 x 6cm (5 x 2½in) gingham side pieces right sides together with the blue star fabric at either side of the base marks. Sew in place.

LITTLE TIP

TO FRAY THE EDGES OF GINGHAM
BENEATH THE FLORAL PATCH,
GENTLY TEASE AWAY THE THREADS
OF FABRIC WITH A PIN.

3 Pin up the sides of the bag so that it looks inside out and machine stitch.

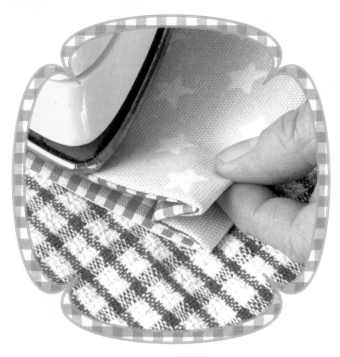

4 Turn through to the right side and press, so that the side panels and base are folded inwards.

5 Fold the 23 x 32cm (9 x 12½in) piece of red gingham in half so that it becomes 23 x 16cm (9 x 6¼in). Pin and sew. This will be the lining.

LITTLE TIP

USE A BRIGHT COLOURED THREAD FOR TACKING SO THAT YOU CAN SEE IT EASILY WHEN YOU UNPICK THE STITCHES.

6 Push the lining fabric into the bag. Fold over the top of the lining at the front and back so that it fits over the top edges of the bag to provide a border. Pin in position and tack to hold in place. Machine stitch, then unpick the tacking stitches.

7 Sew a couple of stitches at the top corners of the bag, to hold the folds of the side panels in place. Stitch a large red button on to the top of the front of the bag, then make a loop out of the thin red ribbon and stitch on to the inside back panel to fasten over the button.

Perfect little pouches

These drawstring bags are far too pretty to hide in a cupboard, so hang them on display for all to see. You can alter the scale of them to make tiny pouches for jewellery or even large laundry bags.

1 Place the top and bottom fabric pieces right sides together along the 42cm (16½in) edge and pin. Machine stitch, open the seam and press flat. Fold in half, then pin and sew the back seam. Open seam and press flat, then position so that it is in the centre back of the bag. Pin and sew the bottom edge of the bag, turn through to the right side and press.

2 Turn under the top edge of the bag by 10cm (4in) and press. Mark 4.5cm (1¾in) down from the top at either side of the bag. Unfold the top edge, then sew buttonholes at each side, placing them 2cm (¾in) down from the marks.

3 Fold over the top edge again and stitch around the top of the bag at the top and bottom of the buttonholes for a channel to thread your drawstring. Cut the gingham ribbon in half and thread these through the buttonholes, using a safety pin. Tie the ends so you have a drawstring.

4 Make a floral patch as described for the cosmetic bag (see page 36) and stitch this on to the front of the bag, to the left-hand side.

Materials

✤ Fabrics:
   ✤ top panel: blue/green, 28 x 42cm (11 x 16½in)
   ✤ bottom panel: pink, 10 x 42cm (4 x 16½in)
   ✤ scraps of floral and gingham fabric

✤ Selection of beads and sequins

✤ Embroidery thread (to match colour scheme)

✤ Gingham ribbon 150cm (59in)

✤ Basic kit (see page 111)

Finished size
20 x 28cm (8 x 11in)

LITTLE TIP
TRY MAKING THESE POUCHES IN PLASTIC-COATED FABRICS TO MAKE WATERPROOF WASH BAGS.

Dotty about you bag

Step out in style with this super cute polka dot bag with bird appliqué. There's a matching purse on page 48 to enhance the look – so sweet, you'll want to make it in different fabrics to match your best outfits. If you search the Internet you'll find a wide choice of purse and bag frames in many different shapes, styles and colours, so choose your favourite and adapt the fabric measurements accordingly.

Small wonder

The bird and cage motif lifts the blue fabric and compliments the vintage style bag frame

Materials

- Fabrics:
    - navy and white polka dot 30 x 40cm (12 x 15¾in)
    - navy lining material 30 x 40cm (12 x 15¾in)
    - scrap of cream satin

- Stitch-on bag frame with clasp and chain 15cm (5¾in) long approx.

- Cream embroidery thread

- Navy blue flower trim 70cm (27½in) approx.

- Basic kit (see page 111)

Finished size

23 x 15cm (9 x 5¾in) approx.

- sizes and fabric measurements are based on a bag frame 15 x 6cm (5¾ x 2½in). Alter measurements to suit your bag frame.

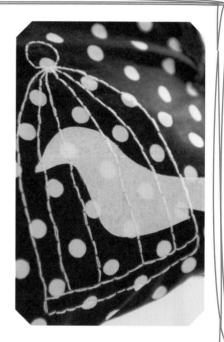

1 Depending on the size of your bag frame, make a paper template for the shape of the bag. Cut out two panels for the front and back of the bag, and another two for the lining, allowing a 1cm (⅜in) seam allowance all the way around.

2 Fold by 1cm (⅜in) and tack the top and side edges that will be sewn on to the frame. Do this on both the front and back panels and the lining pieces.

3 Use the template on page 119 to trace a bird shape on to Bondaweb and roughly cut out. Iron on to the back of the cream satin and cut out carefully. Position on the front panel of the bag, bearing in mind where the cage will go, and iron to fix in place.

LITTLE TIP
AFTER YOU HAVE TACKED THE EDGES THAT WILL BE STITCHED ON TO THE BAG FRAME, CHECK THAT THE FABRIC WILL FIT PERFECTLY IN PLACE.

4 With a fabric pencil, mark out the shape of the cage and bars. Use the cream embroidery thread to sew over these lines in backstitch.

LITTLE TIP

IF YOUR BAG FABRIC IS A BIT FLIMSY, USE IRON-ON STABILISER BACKING TO REINFORCE IT.

5 Pin the two pieces of lining fabric together along the sides and bottom and machine stitch.

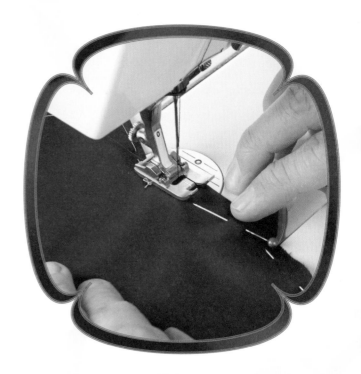

6 Sew the lining on to the bag frame, front and back, then remove tacking stitches. Place the front and back panels of the bag right sides together and pin around the sides and bottom. Machine stitch, turn through to the right side and press.

7 Position on the bag frame so that the lining is tucked inside the bag and sew on to the frame. Remove the tacking stitches. To finish, use fabric glue to stick the navy blue flower trim along the frame edge, covering the stitches.

Dotty about you bag 47

Polka dot purse

Every bag should have a matching purse
and this little one is just big enough for your
pennies. Simple to make, you can easily change
its shape to suit the style of your purse frame.

LITTLE TIP

AFTER STITCHING, SNIP CORNERS
DIAGONALLY TO MAKE TURNING
THROUGH EASIER.

1 Draw around the purse frame and make a paper
template of the shape you want your purse to be.
Leave a 1cm (⅜in) seam allowance all the way around.
Use the template to cut two pieces of polka dot fabric.

2 Use the template on page 119 to draw a flower shape
on to iron-on stabiliser and then iron on to the back
of the cream satin scrap. Cut out and sew to the front panel
of the purse, with a flower cut from the navy flower trim,
a cream bead and a blue seed bead in the middle.

3 Mark the sides where the frame will be and then pin
the purse right sides together and machine stitch
around the sides and bottom from mark to mark. Turn
through to the right side and press flat. Sew the purse on
to the frame with tiny stitches in blue thread.

Materials

❖ Fabrics:
  ❖ navy and white polka
    dot 12 x 25cm
    (4¾ x 10in) approx.
  ❖ scrap of cream satin

❖ Stitch-on purse frame

❖ Navy blue flower trim (scrap)

❖ Iron-on stabiliser backing

❖ Cream bead and blue
  seed bead

❖ Basic kit (see page 111)

Finished size
8 x 10cm (3 x 4in) approx.

Just for the home

Memories in miniature

You can never have too many picture frames, and with these little fabric-covered frames even the smallest snapshots can be beautifully displayed. Be bold with your choice of main patterned print and select simple coordinating fabrics. Add yo-yos made from the main fabric to the corners of each frame to tie the trio together. You can even make a teeny-tiny folding frame to slip into your purse (see page 59).

Small wonder

A trio of frames in coordinating fabrics makes such an attractive display

Materials

- ❖ Fabrics:
  - ❖ bold print
  - ❖ pink spotted
  - ❖ blue spotted
- ❖ Pulp board picture frame blanks x 3
- ❖ Printed papers
- ❖ Ribbons – pink and blue (long enough to go around the inside of the picture frame)
- ❖ Seed beads and sequins
- ❖ Yo-yo maker
- ❖ Basic kit (see page 111)

Finished size

10 x 15cm (4 x 6in)

1 Use a craft knife to carefully cut around the sides and bottom of the frame to separate the back panel if necessary.

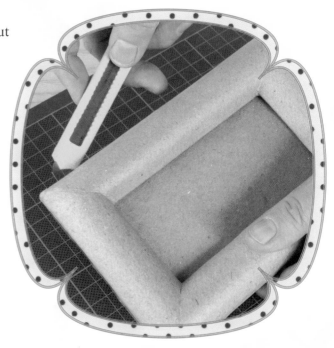

LITTLE TIP

TAKE CARE WHEN USING
A CRAFT KNIFE AS THE BLADE
IS EXTREMELY SHARP.

2 Cut a piece of fabric larger than the frame and draw around the frame on to this fabric using a vanishing pen.

3 When using the bold printed fabric, decorate by adding seed beads and sequins, stitching them around the area that will cover the frame.

4 Draw a cross in the centre of the fabric, to mark out the window of the frame, and cut diagonally from corner to corner to leave four triangular flaps. Use double-sided tape to stick the fabric to the frame. Fold the overhanging fabric over the edges to the back of the frame and secure with more tape.

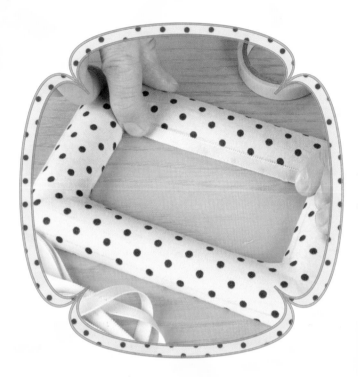

5 Cover the inside edges of the frame with a length of ribbon to hide any raw edges that will appear at the inside corners. Use double-sided tape to stick the ribbon in place.

6 Cut out a piece of coordinating printed paper and stick on to the back panel of the frame using a glue stick.

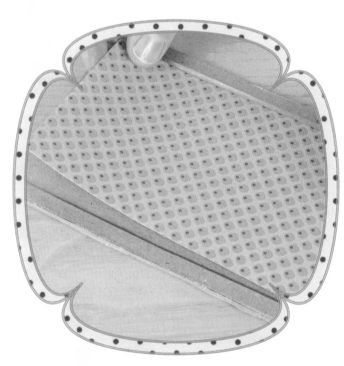

7 Use the bold printed fabric to make three yo-yos for each spotted frame. Cut circles slightly larger than the yo-yo maker.

LITTLE TIP

IF YOU DON'T HAVE A YO-YO MAKER YOU CAN MAKE THEM YOURSELF BY FOLLOWING THE INSTRUCTIONS ON PAGE 118.

8 Place the fabric between the discs of the yo-yo maker and sew (check the instructions that accompany the yo-yo maker). When you've stitched around the circle, remove the fabric from the disc.

9 Gently pull the thread to gather the fabric into a yo-yo shape and then stitch to secure the thread. Press the yo-yo flat with a warm iron. Repeat this process three times in all. In the centre of each yo-yo, sew a large sequin, a smaller one and a seed bead.

LITTLE TIP

WHEN CUTTING OUT THE
SMALL FRAMES TO GO INSIDE
THE BOOKLET ON THE
OPPOSITE PAGE, USE A CRAFT
KNIFE AND CUTTING MAT.

10 Stick the front of the frame to the back along the side and bottom edges using either strong glue or double-sided tape. Arrange three yo-yos in the bottom corner of the frame and secure in place with double-sided tape.

Near and dear

This cute folding frame is tiny enough to tuck into your purse and keep your treasured photos safe. You can also make it much larger so that it can be opened up and displayed in your home.

1 Use masking tape to stick the two pieces of card together so that they fold like a book. Cover with bold fabric, folding the raw edges inside and securing with double-sided tape.

2 Cut a piece of plain coloured paper 6 x 9cm (2½ x 3½in) and stick inside the booklet to cover any raw edges. Cut two frames out of printed paper, each 3.4 x 5cm (1⅜ x 2in), and with a 6mm (¼in) border. Stick inside the booklet, leaving the top edge free from glue so that a tiny photo can slide into place.

3 Put a spot of strong glue on the outside fold of the booklet, half way down, and stick the cream ribbon on so that it can be tied around the booklet to fasten it. Glue a large sequin with a smaller one in the centre to the ribbon at the side.

Materials

❖ Scrap of bold printed fabric

❖ Thick card – two pieces 4.5 x 6cm (1¾ x 2½in)

❖ Masking tape

❖ Thin cream ribbon 25cm (10in)

❖ Heavyweight printed papers – one patterned, one plain

❖ Sequins – one large, one small

❖ Basic kit (see page 111)

Finished size
4.5 x 6cm (1¾ x 2½in)

A jarful of delights

With cute felt flowers springing from the lids, these jars
are so appealing you'll want to make a whole collection
of them to store and display all your beads – much
prettier than keeping them hidden away in plastic tubes.
In keeping with the same theme, you can make the tiny
gift boxes on page 65 for your smallest treasures or
presents for friends, and why not try the sweet little
felt coaster on page 66 as well?

Small wonder

*You don't have to restrict these jars to storing
beads – shells, buttons, candies, almost
anything small and bright would look great*

Materials

- ✤ Mini glass jars with cork stoppers
- ✤ Felt – turquoise, lime, hot pink, cream, lime, orange
- ✤ Seed beads – same colours as above
- ✤ Embroidery threads – same colours as above
- ✤ Mini buttons – various colours
- ✤ Coloured thread – covered wire
- ✤ Basic kit (see page 111)

Finished size
4 x 6cm (1½ x 2½in) approx.

LITTLE TIP

USE SMALL SCISSORS TO CUT OUT THE TINY FLOWERS – DON'T WORRY ABOUT IRREGULAR SHAPES AS IT ADDS TO THE QUIRKINESS.

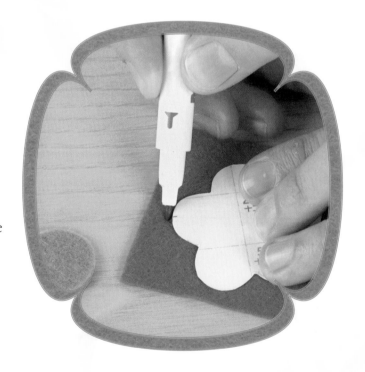

1 Use the template on page 121 to cut out a flower shape in felt (you may have to adjust the size to fit your cork stopper). Trace the centre of the flower on to Bondaweb and iron on to a contrasting coloured felt. Cut out and iron on to the middle of the flower.

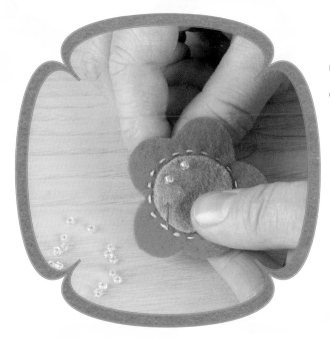

2 Use a brightly coloured embroidery thread, split into two strands, to sew small running stitches around the outside of the circle in the middle of the flower. Sew seed beads on to the centre of the flower.

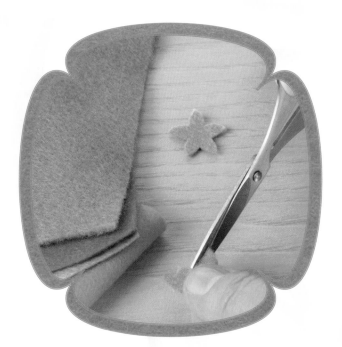

3 Use the templates on page 121 to cut out tiny flower shapes from different coloured felt.

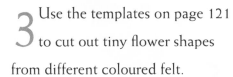

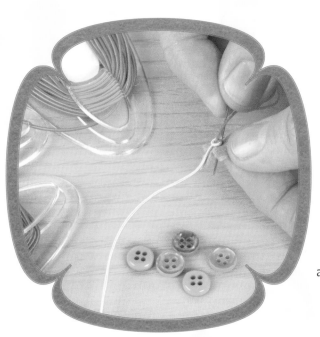

4 Stitch an 8cm (3in) length of thread-covered wire on to the back of one of the felt flowers (make a loop at the top of the wire and stitch through that to stop the wire slipping out of the stitches). Cover this by sewing a button on to both sides of the felt flower at the same time.

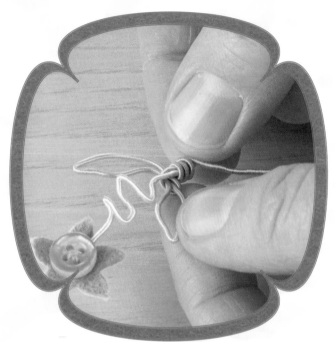

5 Bend and twist the wire into spirals to make the stalk. Add another length of green wire to make leaf shapes. Make a small hole in the centre of the large felt flower, push the ends of the wire through and bend, so that they are flat against the large flower underneath.

6 Make sure that the tiny flower is standing well on the wire and then use strong glue to stick the felt flower on top of the cork stopper.

Box clever

Forget boring gift boxes – these little cuties are ideal to package small gifts for your best friends. Coordinate the colours of felt, ribbon and beads and they'll look great on a dressing table too.

1 Paint the boxes with white acrylic paint and leave to dry. They may need several coats to cover completely.

2 Make felt flowers as described for the bead jars on pages 62–63, adjusting the sizes so that they fit the top of your round boxes. Decorate them with stitching and beads then use strong glue to stick them on to the top of the boxes.

3 Glue a length of pretty ribbon around the side of the lid of the box to finish.

Materials

❖ Tiny round pulp board boxes

❖ White acrylic paint and brush

❖ Felt – various colours

❖ Embroidery thread – various colours

❖ Seed beads

❖ Small lengths of various ribbons

❖ Basic kit (see page 111)

Finished size
4 x 4cm (1½ x 1½in) and 3 x 3cm (1¼ x 1¼in)

LITTLE TIP
WHEN SEWING SEED BEADS, ALWAYS MAKE SURE YOU HAVE A BEADING NEEDLE FINE ENOUGH TO PASS THROUGH THE BEAD BEFORE YOU START.

Flower power

This felt coaster, with its delicate little buttons and petal decorations, is so pretty, especially with a small vase of flowers on top. Go for bright colours and indulge your girliness!

LITTLE TIP

CUT TWO OR THREE DIFFERENT STYLES OF FLOWERS AND ARRANGE THEM ALTERNATELY, MIXING UP THE COLOURS FOR A BALANCED LOOK.

Materials

❖ Felt – various colours

❖ Embroidery thread – various colours

❖ Tiny buttons – various colours

❖ Iron-on stabiliser backing

❖ Basic kit (see page 111)

Finished size
14 x 13.5cm (5½ x 5¼in) approx.

1 Use the template on page 121 to trace the large flower on to the back of iron-on stabiliser, iron on to pink felt and cut out. Trace the centre of the flower on to Bondaweb and iron on to cream felt. Cut out, peel off the paper backing and iron on to the centre of the pink felt flower.

2 Cut out 12 tiny flowers (see templates on page 121) in different coloured felts and stitch them around the edge of the centre of the flower, with a button in the middle of each one.

3 Sew running stitch in between all of the tiny flowers in pink embroidery thread, split into two strands.

Shabby chic at heart

Frayed edges give this mini bed pillow a carefree, romantic look, mixing stripes, checks, spots and florals for a shabby chic, homespun feel. It would look so sweet resting on a patchwork quilt, or nestled in a chair in the corner of the bedroom. Any spare scraps can be used to make a stack of mini scented sachets, which are ideal for adding a touch of style and fragrance to any room

(see page 75).

Small wonder

Embellishing with stray buttons and beads ensures a pick 'n' mix flea-market feel

Materials

- ❖ Selection of coordinating vintage-style fabrics:
  - ❖ back and front – 20cm (8in) square each
  - ❖ patches – at least five different fabric scraps
- ❖ Embroidery threads – a selection to match and contrast with your chosen fabrics
- ❖ Selection of stray beads, buttons and sequins (iridescent sequins look so pretty)
- ❖ Wadding (batting)
- ❖ Basic kit (see page 111)

Finished size
17cm (6½in) square

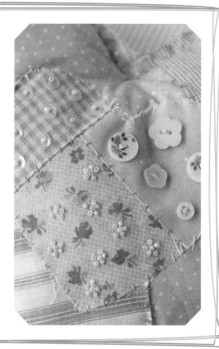

LITTLE TIP

IF YOUR FABRICS LOOK TOO NEAT AND NEW, TRY SOAKING THEM IN A WEAK SOLUTION OF TEA TO GIVE THEM A GENTLY AGED TINT.

1 Trace the template of the large heart shape (page 122) on to paper, pin it to your fabric and cut around it to create one back and one front panel.

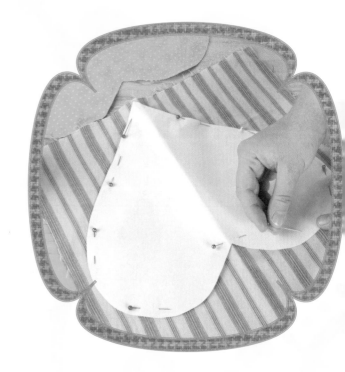

2 Pin patches of different fabrics on to the front panel of the cushion and sew in place with large stitches using a contrast thread. There is no need to hem these first as the soft, frayed edges are part of the cushion's charm.

3 Trace the smaller paper heart-shaped template (page 122) and use it to cut out the smaller inner fabric heart. Pin three patches from different fabrics on to this heart and sew in place, again using large stitches and contrast thread.

4 Use a range of beads and sequins to embellish each patch on the smaller heart. On one patch, sew sequins with a seed bead in the centre, and on a second patch, arrange five seed beads in clusters to make tiny flower shapes.

5 On the third patch of the smaller heart, sew a selection of decorative buttons. Refer to the photograph on page 70 for inspiration.

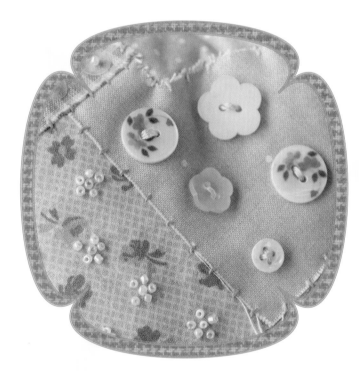

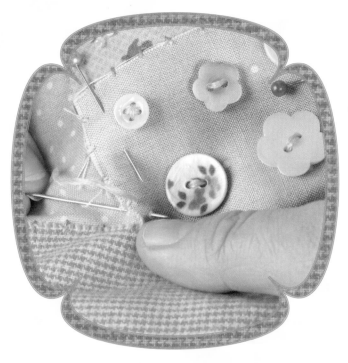

6 Once the small heart has been embellished, pin and sew it on to the centre of the front panel of the cushion, using large stitches.

LITTLE TIP

TO FRAY THE CUSHION EDGES, GENTLY SCRATCH YOUR NAIL ALONG THE EDGE OF THE FABRIC UNTIL STRAY THREADS PULL AWAY.

7 Pin the front and back panels together so that the raw edges are showing. Sew running stitch around the edge of the cushion, leaving a 10cm (4in) gap at the end. Stuff the cushion with wadding (batting) through this gap, then continue sewing to close.

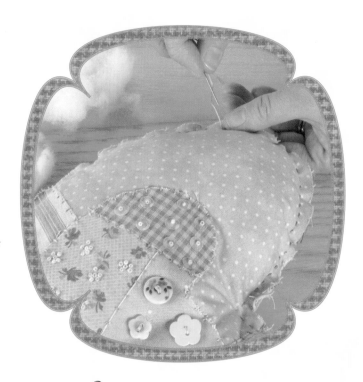

Shabby chic at heart 73

Sweet sachets

Stacked and tied with a ribbon, these little sachets are perfect for adorning your bedside table. Add a few drops of essential oil to the wadding (batting) before stuffing and let the scent fill the room.

LITTLE TIP

TRY USING JEWEL TONED SILKS, SATINS AND VELVETS, WITH PEWTER AND MOTHER-OF-PEARL BUTTONS FOR A MORE SOPHISTICATED, SUMPTUOUS LOOK.

Materials

❖ Fabrics:
  ❖ 2 x 10cm (4in) square
  ❖ 2 x 8cm (3in) square
  ❖ 2 x 6cm (2½in) square
  ❖ scraps for heart

❖ Wadding (batting)

❖ Ribbon – 2 x 25cm (10in) and thin length for heart

❖ Selection of buttons

❖ Basic kit (see page 111)

Finished size
10 x 8cm (4 x 3in) approx.

1 Sew each pair of squares right sides together almost all the way, leaving a 2cm (¾in) gap in each, and turn right side out. Stuff each with wadding (batting) and slipstitch closed.

2 Stack the sachets as shown, and lay the two lengths of ribbon over the top, wrapping them around the stack to meet at the bottom. Stitch to the underside of the bottom sachet. Sew a selection of buttons where the ribbons cross at the top.

3 Make a mini heart sachet, keeping the same raw edges as the bed pillow (see page 70). Attach a thin ribbon and loop over the button on the top of the sachet stack.

Pretty patchwork hangings

Here's a great way to use up all of those tiny scraps of fabric that you can't bear to throw out, or how about recycling some much loved old clothes by cutting them up into smaller pieces? You can add favourites from your button box and some simple wire hearts as well, and mix it all up to make a sweet and simple patchwork plaque that will look fabulous hanging on a wall or door in your home.

Small wonder

Old jeans and cotton shirts work well and the more aged and battered the better

Materials

- ❖ Blank white door plaque 11 x 19cm (4¼ x 7½in) approx.

- ❖ Fabric scraps in red, white and blue – denim, gingham, prints, floral

- ❖ Embroidery thread – red, blue

- ❖ Selection of buttons

- ❖ Wire – thick and thin

- ❖ Thin red ribbon, 50cm (20in)

- ❖ Basic kit (see page 111)

Finished size
11 x 19cm (4¼ x 7½in)

LITTLE TIP

IF YOU DON'T HAVE A BLANK
WALL PLAQUE TO DECORATE,
MAKE ONE BY PAINTING A PIECE
OF MDF OR PLYWOOD WHITE.

1 Draw around your wall plaque on to paper and roughly plan the layout of your patchwork, sketching the position of the individual patches and the wire hearts. Use the template on page 123 for inspiration.

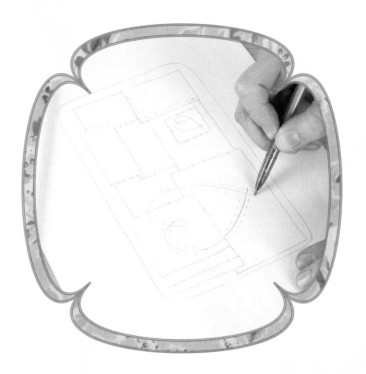

2 Cut out a piece of denim to be the main background fabric. Trace the individual patch shapes on to Bondaweb and iron on to the back of the fabrics that you have chosen. Cut out and position on the denim panel and then iron on to fix in place.

3 Sew the patches on to the denim background using blue and red thread and a variety of large, simple stitches.

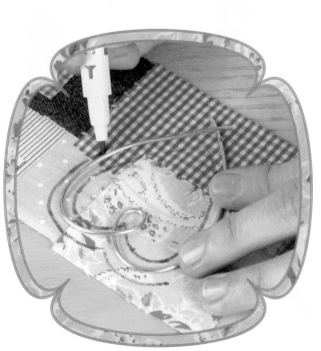

4 Using the templates on page 123, bend the wire hearts into shape, with thicker wire for the large heart and thin for the small heart. Position the large heart on the fabric and draw a line around both the outside and inside edges in vanishing pen. Remove the heart and sew running stitch in red along these lines.

5 Sew both the wire hearts in place using thin white thread so that the stitches are almost invisible. Position the buttons and then sew in place using the blue and red thread.

LITTLE TIP

KEEP THE EDGES OF THE FABRIC RAW, FRAYED AND UNEVEN AND CHOOSE MISMATCHED BUTTONS FOR A SOFT, RAGGEDY LOOK.

6 Tie the red ribbon through the holes at the top of the plaque to make a loop to hang it by. Position the finished panel of fabric on the plaque and use double-sided tape to hold in place.

Door décor

Carry on the patchwork theme to make other little items to hang around the home (see page 83). Door hanger blanks are made in unfinished wood so start with a coat of white acrylic paint.

LITTLE TIP

EMBROIDER A NAME ON TO THE FABRIC TO MAKE IT A PERSONALISED DOOR HANGER FOR A BEDROOM

1 Plan the layout of the patchwork for the hanger on paper. Choose a fabric for the background panel and trace the other patches on to Bondaweb. Cut out the shapes and iron on to the back of the chosen fabrics. Position these shapes on the background fabric, then iron on to hold in place.

2 Sew around the patches with blue and red thread in large stitches. Make a wire heart shape (see page 79) and sew in the centre of the fabric. Sew buttons in place. Stick the finished panel on to the door hanger.

3 Take a small, red, heart-shaped button and sew blue thread through the holes, tying at the back of the button. Glue this button in place at the very top of the hanger.

Materials

❖ Door hanger blank, white

❖ Fabric scraps

❖ White acrylic paint

❖ Thick wire

❖ Embroidery thread – red, blue

❖ Small, red, heart-shaped button and various others

❖ Basic kit (see page 111)

Finished size
9 x 24.5cm (3½ x 9¾in)

Sweetheart hanger

For a romantic touch for a bedroom door and the perfect Valentine's gift, the denim scrap, wire and buttons in this design combine to create a stylish but simple-to-make decoration.

LITTLE TIP

FOR A LOVELY WINDOW DECORATION, TRY THREADING PRETTY BEADS ON TO THE WIRE INSTEAD OF BUTTONS AND LEAVE OUT THE DENIM.

Materials

❖ Denim scrap

❖ Wire – thick and thin

❖ Selection of small white buttons

❖ Thin red ribbon 40cm (15½in)

❖ Basic kit (see page 111)

Finished size
6 x 10cm (2½ x 4in) approx.

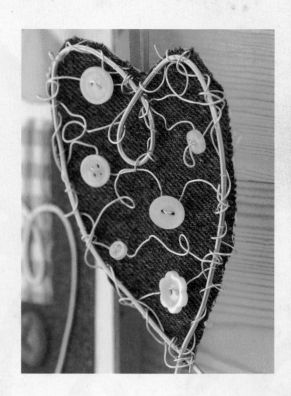

1 Bend the thick wire into the shape of a large heart using the template on page 123. Use the thin wire and wrap it loosely around the outside of the heart, then bend and twist it across the inside of the heart, threading on small buttons here and there – use the photo for inspiration.

2 When the heart is finished, stitch it on to a scrap of denim (sewing around the outside of the heart shape). Cut out the denim so that it is the same shape as the heart. Finish by stitching a loop of thin red ribbon at the top so that it can be hung.

Little basket of goodies

Old fashioned sewing baskets have a fantastic retro feel and are, of course, so useful if you love to sew (and if you're reading this, you must!). Choose a picnic hamper style basket, cover it with cheerful gingham fabric and fill with red strawberries to keep your pins and needles safe (see pages 90–91). The polka dot ribbon is a simple way of securing the lining, as well as being super-cute and the strawberry tag completes the look.

Small wonder

Gingham fabric is so reminiscent of picnics; you can almost smell the strawberries...

Materials

- ✤ Fabrics:
  - ✣ red gingham 50 x 80cm (20 x 31½in) approx. (depending on size of basket)
  - ✣ felt – red, green
- ✤ Mini picnic style basket
- ✤ Rubber band
- ✤ Red spotted ribbon 1m (39¼in) approx.
- ✤ Thin red ribbon 20cm (8in)
- ✤ Green and white striped brad
- ✤ Basic kit (see page 111)

Finished size
16 x 24cm (6¼ x 9½in) approx.

LITTLE TIP

TACK THE GINGHAM FABRIC
PIECES TOGETHER AND CHECK
IT FITS INTO THE BASKET BEFORE
SEWING PROPERLY.

1 Make a paper template the same size as the inside bottom of your basket. Pin on to the gingham fabric and cut around, leaving a 1cm (⅜in) seam allowance.

2 Measure the circumference of the basket, add 4cm (1½in) and divide by two. Measure the depth of the basket and double. Use these measurements to cut two pieces of gingham fabric for the side panels. Pin and sew these pieces on to the bottom panel so that the side seams will be at the halfway point on the bottom panel.

3 Pin and sew up the side seams, stopping to allow the handle to come through. Hem the top edge.

4 Place the fabric inside the basket, folding the edges over the outside. They should overlap by about 5cm (2in). Secure in place with a rubber band.

5 Tie a length of spotted red ribbon around the basket to hide the rubber band and finish with a bow.

6 Use the templates on page 124 to cut a strawberry shape out of red felt and a leaf out of green felt. Place the leaf on to the top of the strawberry.

Use the templates on page 124

LITTLE TIP

IF THE EDGES OF THE BASKET LINING HANG TOO LOW, SIMPLY FOLD UNDER THE EDGE TO THE RIGHT LENGTH AND HEM.

7 Loop the thin red ribbon around the handle of the basket and fasten on to the strawberry and leaf using a striped brad, so that it makes a tag.

Little basket of goodies 89

Pins and needles

No sewing kit is complete without a pincushion and this strawberry-shaped one looks good enough to eat. The matching case means you'll never have to hunt around for a needle again.

LITTLE TIP

IF YOU CAN'T FIND MATCHING BRADS, JUST USE RED AND GREEN BUTTONS. YOU COULD EVEN COVER YOUR OWN (SEE PAGE 26).

Materials

❖ Felt – red 10 x 18cm (4 x 7in), green (scrap)

❖ Green embroidery thread

❖ Red checked brad

❖ Basic kit (see page 111)

Finished size

7 x 8.5cm (2¾ x 6½in) approx.

Needle Case

1 Cut two strawberry shapes out of red felt using the template on page 124, and a leaf shape out of green felt. Use green embroidery thread to sew the two red pieces together along the top edge using running stitch. Continue sewing running stitch around the front piece only, until you're back to the start.

2 With green thread, sew lines on to the leaf in backstitch in the same way as for the pin cushion and attach a red checked brad to the centre. Sew the leaf on to the top of the strawberry. Open up the strawberry and push needles into the back panel to store.

Pincushion

1 Use the template on page 124 to cut two strawberry shapes out of red fabric, adding a 1cm (⅜in) seam allowance. Pin the pieces right sides together and sew around the edges, leaving the top edge open.

2 Turn through to the right side and press. Stuff firmly with wadding (batting) and then sew up the opening.

3 Use the template on page 124 to cut out a leaf shape in green felt, and sew lines radiating from the centre in green backstitch. Attach a spotted brad in the centre of the leaf. Sew the leaf on to the strawberry.

Materials

❖ Red cotton fabric
14 x 20cm (5½ x 8in)

❖ Green felt scrap

❖ Wadding (batting)

❖ Green spotted brad

❖ Green embroidery thread

❖ Basic kit (see page 111)

Finished size
7 x 8.5cm (2¾ x 6½in) approx.

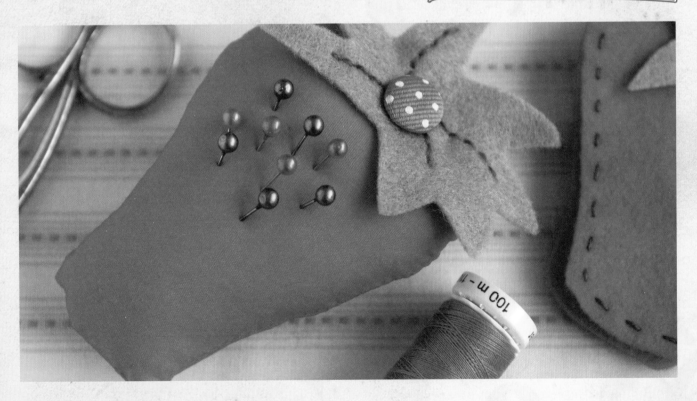

Hung up with style

Covered hangers are a definite retro favourite, with a hint of kitsch thrown in. These ones would look gorgeous in a little girl's wardrobe and make a wonderful birthday gift. For a coordinated look, stick to one colour scheme but use a different print for each hanger and decorate individually with trims, seed beads and little ready-made satin flowers. They are so pretty it almost seems a shame to hide them with clothes!

Small wonder

Mini satin flowers are embellished with felt and a seed bead to create the perfect finishing touch

Materials

- ✤ Small wooden coat hangers with hooks that can be removed

- ✤ Pink cotton fabrics – floral, checked, gingham – approx. 50 x 25cm (20 x 10in) each

- ✤ Trims – pom-pom, beaded, crocheted, approx. 50cm (20in) each

- ✤ Felt – pink, green

- ✤ Seed beads – pink, clear

- ✤ Mini satin flowers

- ✤ Basic kit (see page 111)

Finished size
16 x 32cm (6¼ x 12¼in) approx.

1 Remove the hook and place the hanger on a double-layered piece of fabric. Use a vanishing pen to draw around the hanger, leaving a seam allowance of about 1.5cm (½in).

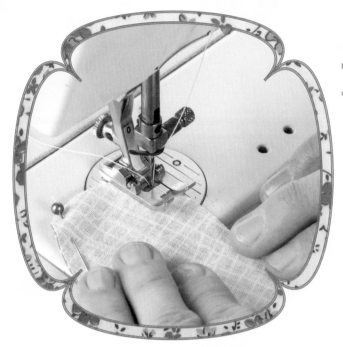

2 Cut out the drawn shape so that you have two pieces of fabric and pin right sides together. Machine stitch, leaving one end open.

3 Carefully turn through to the right side through the open end and press flat.

LITTLE TIP

FOR A LITTLE BOY'S WARDROBE, CHANGE THE COLOUR SCHEME TO BLUE AND USE A MIXTURE OF DENIM AND CHECKED FABRIC WITHOUT THE TRIMS.

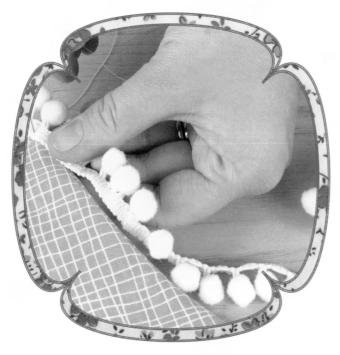

4 Hand-stitch a length of trimming to the bottom edge of the cover.

LITTLE TIP

WHEN SEWING THE TRIM IN PLACE, USE THE SAME COLOURED THREAD AND VERY TINY STITCHES SO THAT THEY ARE HARD TO SEE.

5 Cut leaf shapes out of green felt and sew these on to a small scrap of pink felt. Stitch a mini satin flower, with a seed bead in the centre, in place on the pink felt. Alternatively, sew a cluster of three flowers on to the felt. Trim away any excess pink felt so it's hidden beneath the flowers and leaves.

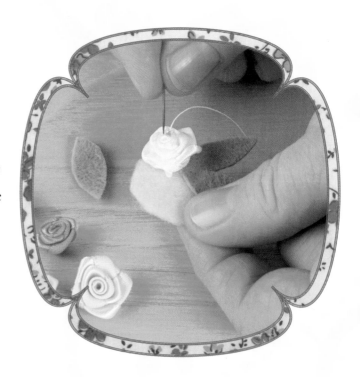

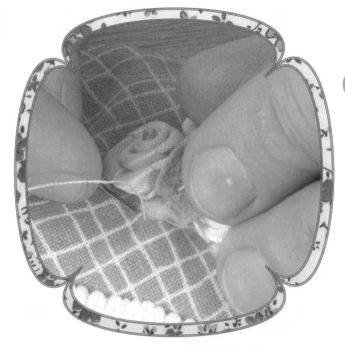

6 Slide the cover on to the hanger, make a small hole in the top seam to allow the hook to be attached and mark the centre point of the cover. Remove the hook and take the cover off the hanger again. Stitch the flowers on to the cover on top of the centre mark.

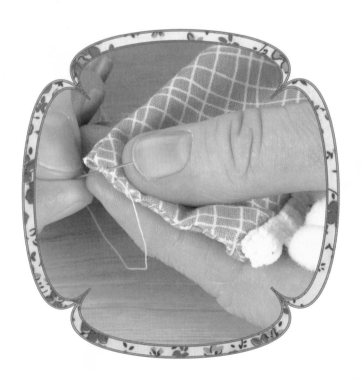

7 Slide the cover back on to the hanger, attach the hook and sew up the opening at the end of the cover.

Heaven scent

Loop these lavender-filled hearts over your hangers and let the aroma fill your wardrobe. Or stuff the hearts with wadding (batting) and add a few drops of perfume instead.

LITTLE TIP

WHEN TURNING THE HEART
THROUGH TO THE RIGHT SIDE,
USE A POINT LIKE A PENCIL TO
PUSH THE BOTTOM OF THE HEART
OUT FULLY.

1 Use the template on page 123 to cut out two hearts from different pieces of fabric. Trace the inner heart shape on to Bondaweb and iron on to the back of a third fabric. Cut out and iron to the centre of a larger heart.

2 Sew around the inner heart in pink running stitch and stitch a pink button to the centre. Pin the right sides of the front and back panels of the heart together and machine stitch, leaving a gap to allow for filling.

3 Turn through and press flat. Fill with dried lavender or whatever is desired and carefully sew up the gap. Make a loop with the ribbon and sew on to the front of the heart at the top, covering the stitches with a tiny green button.

Materials

❖ Pink cotton fabrics – floral, gingham, checked, 15 x 25cm (6 x 10in) each approx.

❖ Buttons – 3 x medium sized pink, 3 x tiny lime green

❖ Embroidery thread – hot pink

❖ Pink ribbon – 40cm (15½in) per heart

❖ Dried lavender or small scented flowers to fill

❖ Basic kit (see page 111)

Finished size
10 x 8cm (4 x 3in) approx.

Treasure chest

Transform a mini wooden chest of drawers into something special using little scraps of your favourite pieces of fabric to cover the front and top of the drawers. Pretty flower decorations, sewn from coordinating fabrics, make an eye-catching finishing touch. With buttons for handles, what better place to house the rest of your collection, or any other treasures you need to keep safe?

Small wonder

You can adapt this design to fit any style of small drawers. Why not try covering small boxes to match?

Materials

- ✤ Wooden mini drawers
- ✤ Cotton fabrics – a different one for each drawer, plus one for the top, all coordinating colours (size depends on size of drawers)
- ✤ Embroidery threads in similar colours to fabrics
- ✤ Oval shell buttons (one for each drawer plus an extra one)
- ✤ Small shell buttons x 3
- ✤ Small buttons (one for each drawer)
- ✤ Tiny wooden square beads (one for each drawer)
- ✤ Iron-on stabiliser backing
- ✤ Scrap of felt
- ✤ Basic kit (see page 111)

Finished size
10 x 28cm (4 x 11in) approx. depending on size of your drawers

1 Remove the wooden handles from the drawers and, if necessary, drill small holes to fit new handles. Also, drill a small hole at the top back panel of the drawers.

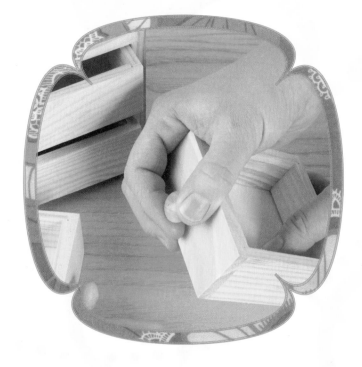

2 Make a paper template the same size as the front of your drawers and use it to cut panels of fabric, one for each drawer, leaving a 1cm (⅜in) hem allowance. Fold under the edges of the panels, press flat and pin.

3 Sew around the edges of the panels in coordinating embroidery thread using running stitch. When all of the panels are complete, stick on to the front of the drawers using strong glue and leave to dry completely.

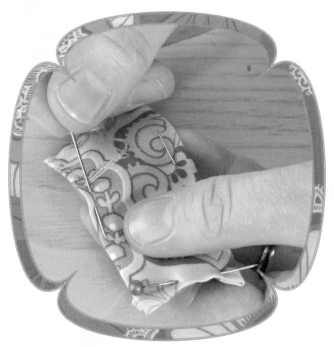

LITTLE TIP

WHEN CHOOSING FABRICS
REMEMBER THAT THE PIECES USED
ARE VERY SMALL SO LARGE PRINTS
MAY NOT BE CLEARLY SEEN.

4 Make button handles for each drawer by threading embroidery thread (split into three strands) from the back of the drawer, through a small button and out to the front. Thread a small square bead and then add a larger oval button. Sew the button in place, threading back through the square bead and the small button at the back of the drawer.

5 Tie the thread securely to hold in place. Make sure you tie the button handles on as tightly as possible to prevent them from drooping.

6 Make a paper template the same size as the top of the drawers, and use this to cut a panel of fabric, again leaving a 1cm (³⁄₈in) hem allowance.

7 Fold under the edges and press. Pin and sew around the edges in running stitch. Use strong glue to stick this panel on to the top of the drawers. Leave to dry.

8 Use the template on page 125 to cut out ten petal shapes from leftover fabrics used for the drawers. Place two petals of the same fabric right sides together and sew around the edges leaving the bottom open. Turn through to the right side and press. Make five petals in all.

9 Sew the five petals in a flower shape on to a tiny scrap of felt. Use the template on page 125 to draw a small flower shape on to iron-on stabiliser and iron on to the back of a coordinating fabric. Cut out and sew in place in the centre of the petals using tiny running stitches following the shape of the small flower. Attach to the top of the drawers as in step 4. Tie the threads tightly at the back.

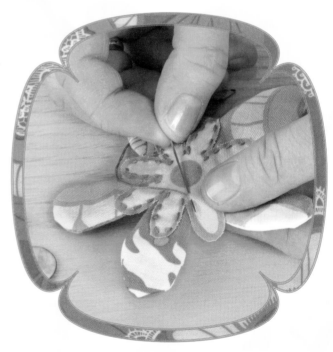

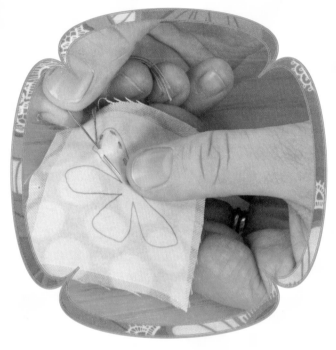

10 Using the template on page 125, trace three small flowers on to iron-on stabiliser and iron on to the back of a different fabric. Sew around the edges of these flowers in tiny running stitches. Cut out and sew a small shell button on to the centre of each.

LITTLE TIP

WHEN STICKING THE SMALL FLOWERS ON TO THE TOP OF THE DRAWERS, PUT A DOT OF GLUE IN THE CENTRE ONLY, SO THAT THE PETALS CAN CURL UP.

11 To finish off, stick these three flowers in place on to the top of the drawers using textile or other strong glue.

Dishy delight

This little trinket dish would look so cute on any dressing table and is a lovely way to use up your favourite fabrics. Choose carefully, so that you pick the four that go together best.

1 Use the template on page 125 to trace the larger shape on to iron-on stabiliser backing. Cut out and iron on to the back of a patterned fabric. Cut the patterned fabric so it is 1cm (⅜in) larger than the original shape all the way around. Fold in the fabric edges and press flat.

2 Trace the smaller shape on page 125 on to Bondaweb, iron to a different fabric and cut out. Peel off the backing and place on top of the larger shape so it covers the folded edges. Iron in place. Fold up the sides of the dish and sew together at the side seams with tiny stitches.

3 With the two patterned scraps, use Bondaweb to stick the same fabrics together, so that you have two pieces, each with the same print on either side. Use the templates on page 125 to cut four small flowers from one piece, and one larger flower from the other. Sew the small flowers to the corners of the dish, securing in place with a button. Sew the larger flower in the centre of the dish with a button in the middle.

Materials

❖ Fabrics:
  ❖ 2 x 20cm (8in) square
  ❖ scraps of two other patterns
❖ Iron-on stabiliser backing
❖ Shell buttons x 5
❖ Embroidery thread
❖ Basic kit (see page 111)

Finished size
11 x 11 x 3cm (4¼ x 4¼ x 1in)

LITTLE TIP
MAKE A SIMPLE, SMALL CUSHION OUT OF THE SAME FABRICS AND DECORATE WITH A CLUSTER OF THE SMALL FLOWERS USED ON THE TRINKET DISH.

Techniques

Basic kit

As well as the specific items described in the Materials section of each project, this basic sewing kit includes everything else you will need to make your little luxuries.

1 Iron
You will need an iron and an ironing surface for using Bondaweb (see below) and pressing fabrics and seams.

2 Fabric markers and pencils
Vanishing markers are ideal, as they disappear after several hours on their own, or with a little water. Use fabric pencils or tailors' chalk to draw a line or pattern. The marks rub off once the stitching is complete.

3 Pins
Use pins when joining fabrics to keep the pieces together before sewing.

4 Craft knife, cutting mat and ruler
Use for cutting out paper to give a much cleaner, more accurate cut than scissors. You will also need a ruler for measuring or marking out the lines on the fabric.

5 Tape measure
Handy for measuring long lengths.

6 Bondaweb
This comes in a roll or in pre-cut pieces, also known as Wonderweb, and looks like paper. It is used for attaching two pieces of fabric together for easy appliqué: one side can be drawn on and the other has a thin membrane of glue, which melts when heated by an iron (see page 113).

7 Glue
Textile or fabric glue is essential for attaching ribbons, braids and lengths of sequins where you don't want to see stitching. Strong glue (such as PVA) is used for sticking fabrics to other surfaces, such as wood or plastic.

8 Double-sided tape
This is a neat alternative to glue, e.g. for attaching the fabric cover to the notebook in Keeping a note (page 10).

9 Scissors
Embroidery scissors have small, sharp blades, ideal for cutting thread. Use dressmaking scissors for cutting fabric.

10 Needles
Hand, beading and machine needles are available in many sizes. Choose a needle that matches the thickness of the thread you are using, so the thread passes easily through the fabric. Use an appropriate machine needle for your work and change it frequently – immediately if damaged or bent.

11 Sewing and embroidery thread
Good quality cotton thread is easy to cut and sew and doesn't fray too readily. Use a strong thread when attaching beads and sequins. Embroidery thread, for decorative stitching, is made up of thin strands (usually six). If this is too thick to work with, you can split the thread into two or three strands.

12 Sewing machine
A sewing machine will produce much stronger seams than hand sewing and is a lot quicker and easier. If you haven't access to a sewing machine, hand sewing will suffice for all these projects as they are small enough and will not be subject to heavy loads.

Working with fabric

Before you begin to sew, it pays to spend a little time preparing your material. Here are some techniques that will stand you in good stead when making the projects in this book – and many more besides.

Pinning

This may seem rather obvious, but if you pin fabric correctly before sewing then it can make it a lot easier to stitch.

Pinning edges and hems

1 Fold the edge of the fabric over and press with an iron. Fold a second time to hide any raw edges and then press again.

2 Place the pins along the edge so that the end of the pin is at the right-hand side. This means that you can pull the pins out easily as you stitch.

Pinning fabrics together

When pinning two fabrics together you can use the basic technique above, or this one, which delivers better results especially if the fabrics are slippery or stretchy.

1 Place the fabrics together edge to edge. Pin at right angles to the edge to the fabrics, leaving a small gap between the pins. If using a sewing machine, you can sew straight over the pins (go fairly slowly) and remove them at the end.

IRON-ON STABILISER

IF YOUR FABRIC IS A LITTLE FLIMSY, USE IRON-ON STABILISER BACKING. THIS IS A THIN MEMBRANE THAT STICKS TO THE BACK OF FABRIC WHEN IRONED ON, TO ADD EXTRA STRENGTH. IT PREVENTS FRAYED EDGES IF ATTACHED BEFORE CUTTING OUT YOUR SHAPE.

Tacking

Tacking fabrics together is an easy way of making sure that they stay in place as you sew them. As the stitches are removed at the end, they needn't be neat.

1 Using a thin thread in a contrasting colour, sew the fabrics together using large running stitches, without a knot at the end.

2 Once the fabrics have been sewn together with a sewing machine, use a 'quick-unpick' tool or a pin to pull out the tacking stitches.

Marking fabrics

It can help to mark out designs on to your fabrics before stitching so that you can be sure to get it the way you want it.

1 One method is to use a vanishing pen, which will disappear either on its own or with a little water. Use the pen to draw the line you want to follow with stitching. Once stitched, dab with a little water on your finger to remove any traces of the pen.

2 A second method is to use a fabric pencil or tailors' chalk, which will just rub off. Draw the line or pattern with the pencil, taking care not to rub it out as you stitch. Once the stitching is complete, rub the pencil marks to remove.

Using Bondaweb

Appliqué is the name for fabric shapes being stitched on to other fabrics. The easiest way to do this is using a product called Bondaweb (sometimes known as Wonderweb), see page 111.

1 Trace the shape that you want on to the paper side of the Bondaweb (remember the shape will come out in reverse). Cut roughly around and iron on to the back of the fabric that you wish to appliqué.

2 Carefully cut out the shape. Peel off the paper backing, place the shape on to the backing fabric and iron to fix in position.

Hand stitching

All of the hand stitching in this book is very easy to do; simply follow the instructions below for all the stitches that you will need.

Running stitch

This can be used to sew two pieces of fabric together and for decoration, e.g. around the felt flowers in the Funky floral jewellery set, page 18. Start by tying a small knot at the end of your thread. Push the needle from the back of the fabric through to the front. Make a small stitch and push the needle up again, leaving a gap about the same length as the actual stitches. Begin your second stitch in the same way. Pull the thread right through and repeat.

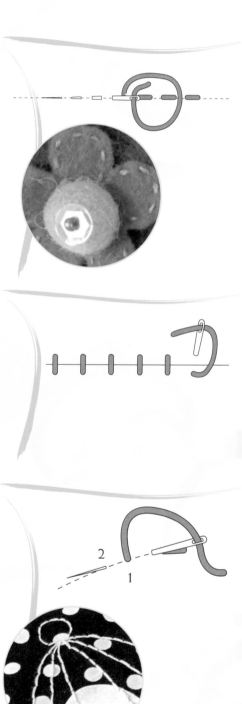

Catch stitch

I use this stitch to sew one piece of fabric to another when using appliqué. Tie a knot at the end of the thread and push up from the back of the fabric to the front, near the join of the two fabrics. Make a small stitch that overlaps the two fabrics in a straight line. Push the needle back through to the back of the fabric, then through to the front of the fabric a little way along from the first stitch and repeat.

Backstitch

Backstitch is used to create a continuous line of stitching, e.g. to make the bird cage in the 'Dotty about you bag', p42. To work backstitch, bring the needle out at the beginning of the stitching line, take a medium-length straight stitch and bring the needle out slightly further along the stitching line (1). Insert the needle at the end of the first stitch and bring it out slightly further still along the stitching line (2). Continue to create a line of joined stitches.

Blanket stitch

Use a blanket stitch to create a decorative edging, such as around the birds' wings in Keeping a note, page 10. Working from left to right, insert the needle into the fabric a little way from the edge, leaving the loose thread running down over the edge at right angles to it. Take the threaded end over the loose end and insert the needle a little way along at the same distance from the edge as before; pass the needle through the loop of thread and gently pull up the thread.

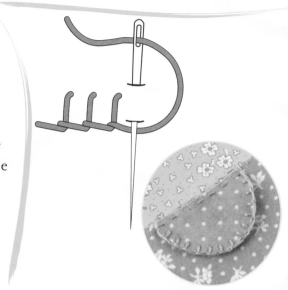

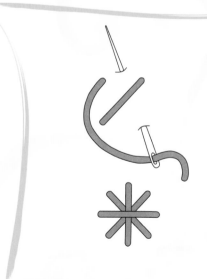

Chain stitch

Bring the needle up through the fabric (**1**). Insert it in the same hole (**2**), forming a loop of thread as you do so, and bring the needle up in the loop (**3**). Pull the thread gently to make the first loop of the chain (**4**). Repeat, keeping the loops rounded (**5**). Finish the last loop of the chain with a small stitch.

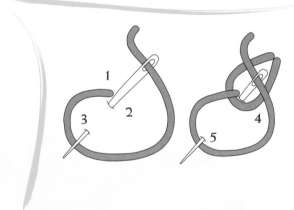

Star stitch

You can make the star as small as you like and it is ideal to use as a flower motif, perhaps in the centre of a covered button (see page 26). Push the needle up through the front of the fabric and down through it, then bring the needle out to one side to make a stitch over the first one, forming a cross. Work the other diagonals in the same way until you have a star with eight points.

Embellishments

Stitching on a few well-chosen embellishments can make the world of difference to your creations, adding colour and texture. You can probably find a button, bead or sequin in any style or shape you care to imagine to make your little luxuries ultra desirable.

Buttons

Buttons can either be used as a practical fastening or as a fun and versatile embellishment to jazz up your designs. You can sew two-holed or four-holed buttons, either using two straight stitches or in a cross. Often it's good to mix two-holed and four-holed buttons together and stitch them on in different ways for a varied look.

LITTLE TIP
TAKE CARE CHOOSING BUTTONS, NOTING THE SHAPE, COLOUR AND NUMBER OF HOLES IN THE BUTTON (TWO OR FOUR).

Always keep your eye out for pretty, individual buttons that can be mixed and matched as decoration.

Sewn on to felt petals with contrasting thread, buttons make perfect little flower centres to brighten up your projects.

Buttons can also be practical and make great little handles for the chest of drawers (page 100).

Beads

Beads look fantastic as a decoration and come in such a variety of colours that you'll find some to suit any fabric that you choose. If you're using tiny seed beads, make sure you have a very fine beading needle, as normal needles may not fit through the hole in the bead.

LITTLE TIP

TIP BEADS INTO THE LID OF A JAR BEFORE YOU START TO STOP THEM ROLLING ABOUT.

1 To stitch on a bead, simply thread your beading needle with fine thread, preferably in the same colour as the bead, and tie a knot at the end. Push the needle through the fabric from back to front at the point that you want the bead to be.

Cluster seed beads together to give great texture and interest to a covered button, see Out of the button box (page 26).

Jazz up the Funky ring (page 23) even more with seed beads. Place one in the centre of a sequin to hide stitches and add sparkle.

2 Thread the bead on to the needle and pull the thread through, then push the needle back through the same point that it entered.

Sequins

Sequins will always add a little sparkle to your design. You can stitch them on individually, but you will be able to see the thread, so make sure that you sew carefully. Alternatively, you can sew them with a seed bead in the centre, which looks neater, without visible stitches.

LITTLE TIP

ARRANGE ALL THE PIECES ON TO YOUR DESIGN BEFORE STITCHING, OR MAKE A SIMPLE SKETCH.

You can use sequins to highlight aspects of a fabric, as with the floral patch on the Cute cosmetic case (page 34).

Making yo-yos

Little fabric yo-yos make such pretty decorations and really brighten up the little picture frames in Memories in miniature (page 52). If you don't have a yo-yo maker, you can easily make them in the following way.

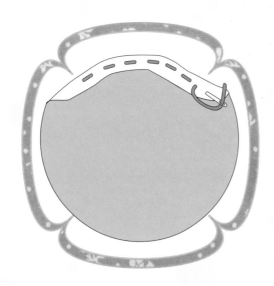

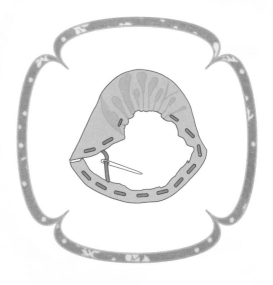

1 Cut a circle of fabric approximately 20cm (8in) in diameter. Fold the edge by 5mm (¼in) and sew running stitch around the circle.

2 When you have reached your start point, gently pull the thread to gather up the edge.

3 Once fully gathered, secure the thread with a small stitch and then press the yo-yo flat with an iron.

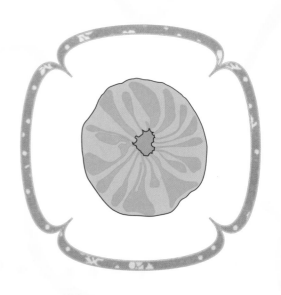

Templates

The following are templates for some of the projects. Simply trace around the shape, pin it on to the fabric and then cut out. Alternatively, draw around the template on to the fabric before cutting out. All the templates are shown here at actual size (100%) for the projects in the book, but you can easily enlarge or reduce them on a photocopier – or simply use them as a guideline and draw your own.

Funky floral jewellery set (pages 18–25)

outer and inner

flowers for bracelet

outer and inner flowers for ring

LITTLE TIP

WHEN TRACING THE SHAPES
ON TO BONDAWEB REMEMBER
THAT THE FINISHED IMAGE
WILL BE REVERSED.

Out of the button box (page 32)

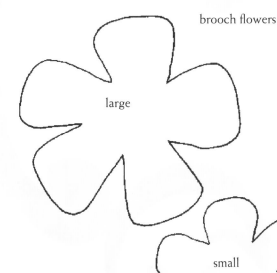

brooch flowers

large

small

Dotty about you bag (pages 42–49)

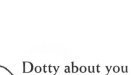

bird

flower for purse

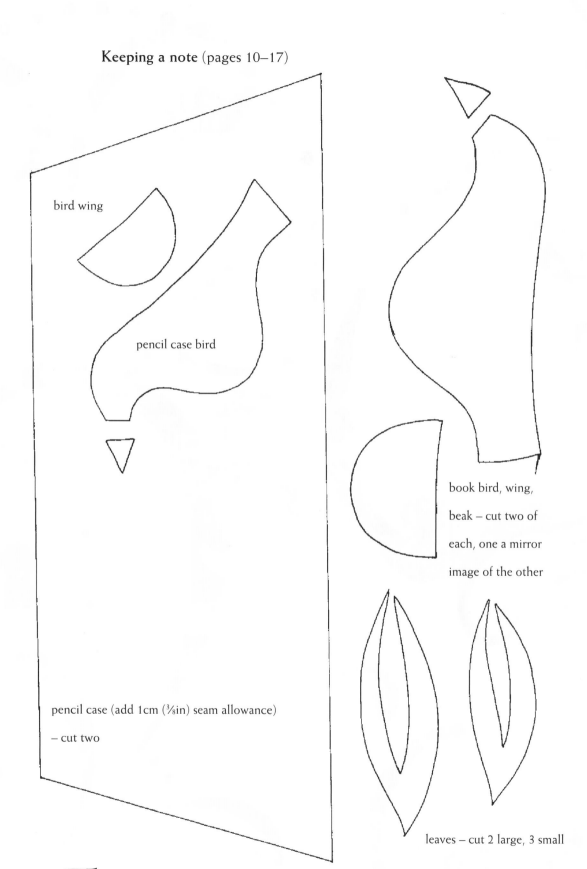

bird wing

pencil case bird

pencil case (add 1cm (⅜in) seam allowance)
– cut two

book bird, wing,

beak – cut two of

each, one a mirror

image of the other

leaves – cut 2 large, 3 small

A jarful of delights (pages 60–67)

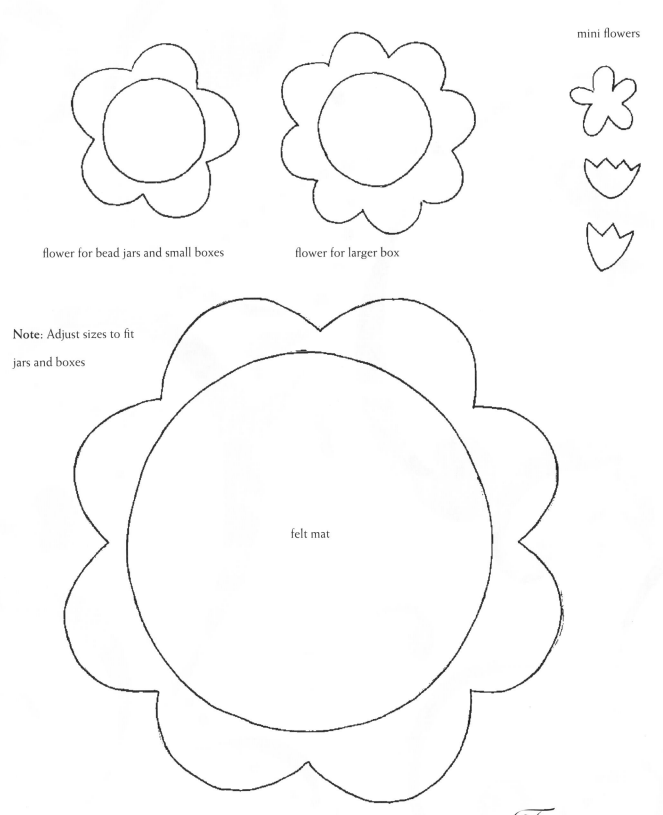

mini flowers

flower for bead jars and small boxes

flower for larger box

Note: Adjust sizes to fit jars and boxes

felt mat

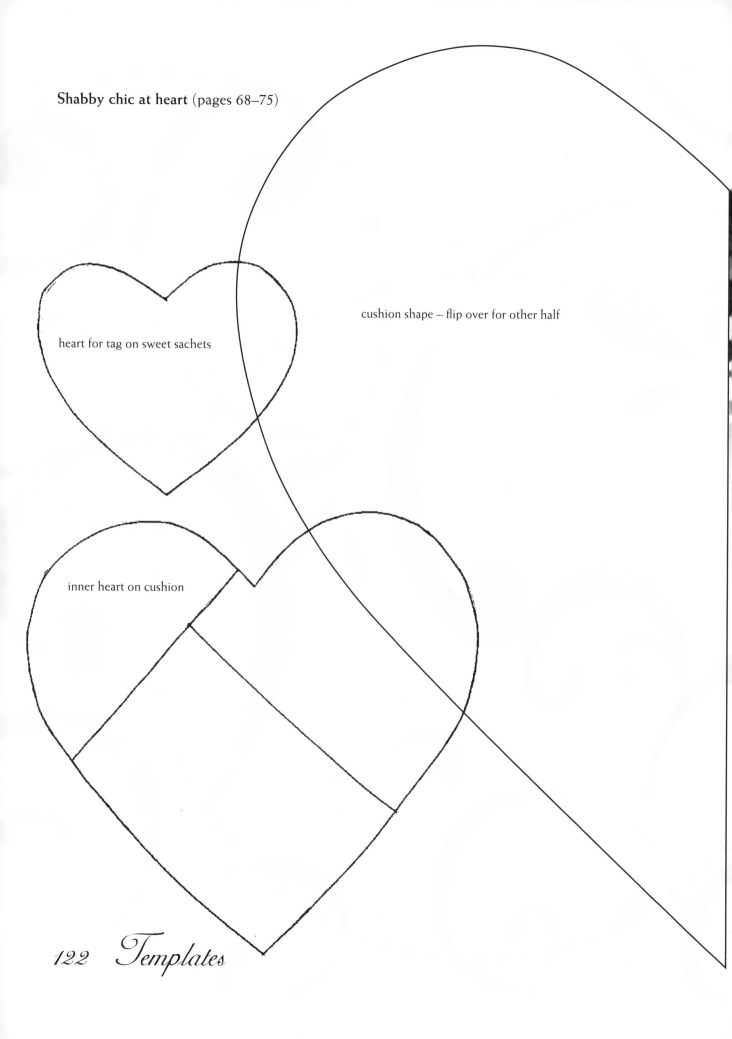

Shabby chic at heart (pages 68–75)

heart for tag on sweet sachets

cushion shape – flip over for other half

inner heart on cushion

Pretty patchwork hangings (pages 76–83)

patchwork and heart shapes for door plaque

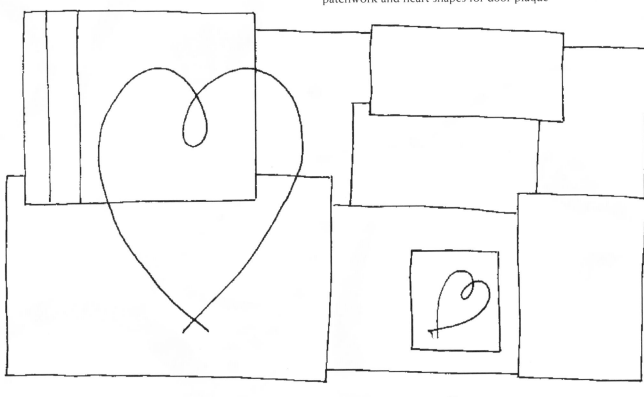

Hung up with style (pages 92–99)

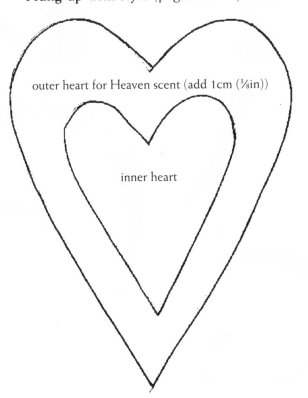

outer heart for Heaven scent (add 1cm (⅜in))

inner heart

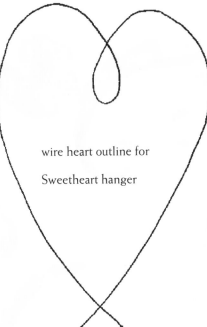

wire heart outline for

Sweetheart hanger

Templates **123**

Little basket of goodies (pages 84–91)

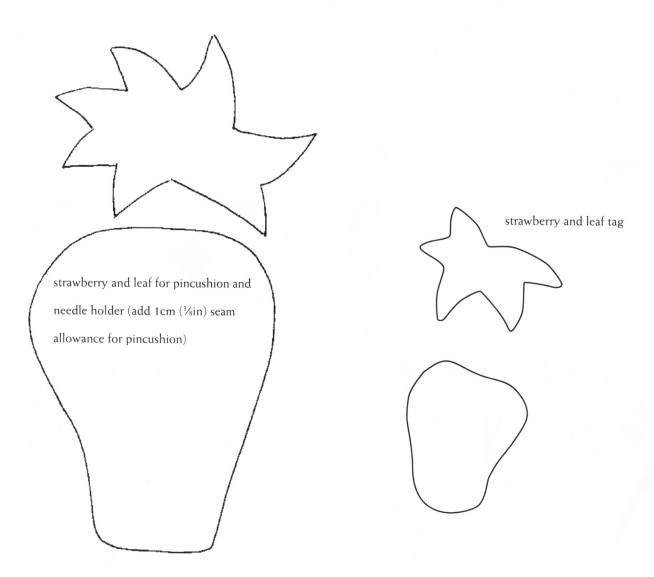

strawberry and leaf for pincushion and
needle holder (add 1cm (⅜in) seam
allowance for pincushion)

strawberry and leaf tag

Treasure chest (pages 100–109)

flowers for top of

drawers – cut three

petals for drawers
– cut ten

large flower for top

of drawers and centre

of dish

flowers for corners of

dish – cut four

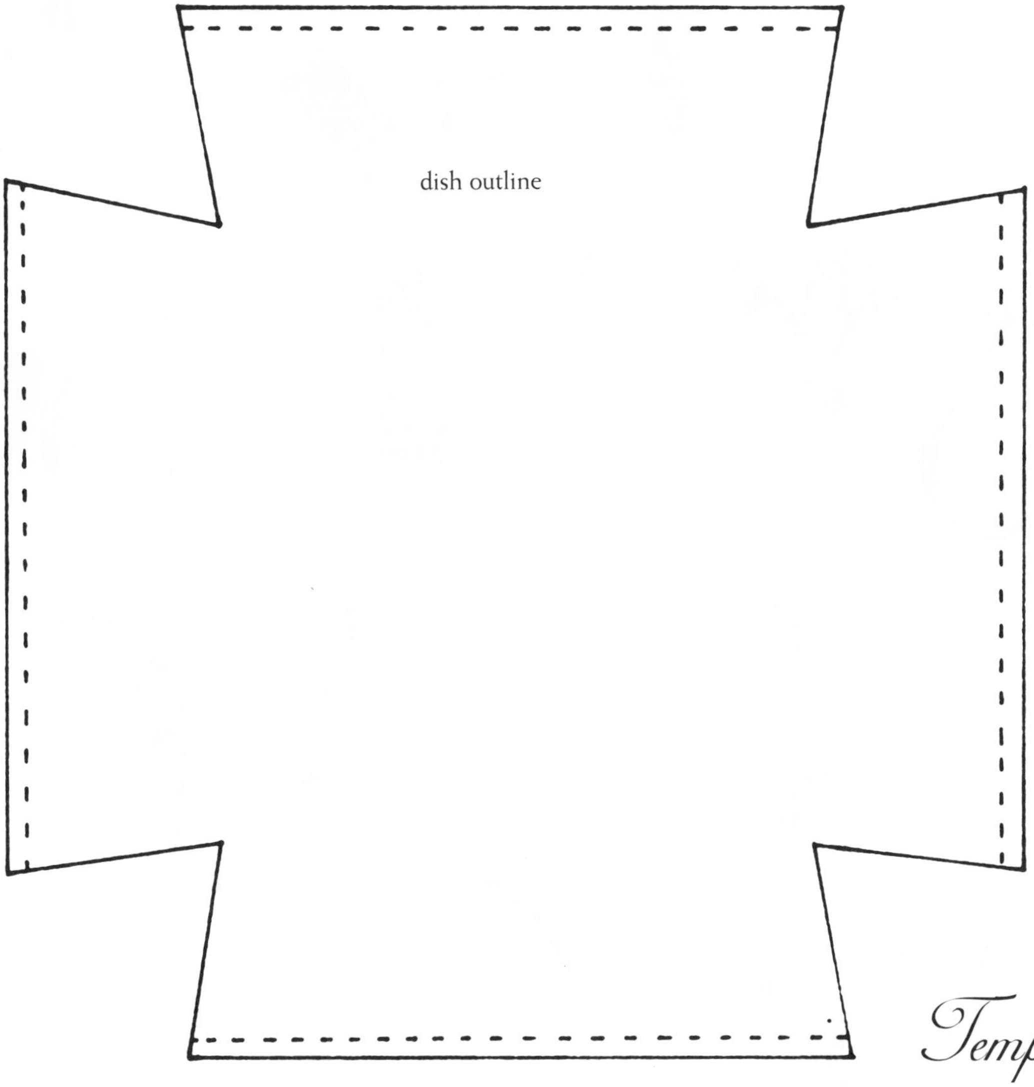

dish outline

Suppliers

UK

The Bead Merchant
PO Box 5025
Coggleshall
Essex, CO6 1HW
Tel: 01376 563567
www.beadmerchant.co.uk

The Cotton Patch
1283–1285 Stratford Road
Hall Green
Birmingham, B28 9AJ
Tel: 0121 702 2840
www.cottonpatch.co.uk

Cath Kidston
Nationwide chain of stores
Tel: 08450 262 440
www.cathkidston.co.uk

Crafty Ribbons
3 Beechwood Clump Farm
Tin Pot Lane, Blandford
Dorset, DT11 7TD
Tel: 01258 455889
www.craftyribbons.com

Fred Aldous Ltd
37 Lever Street
Manchester, M1 1LW
Tel: 0161 236 4224
www.fredaldous.co.uk

Gütermann Beads
Perivale-Gütermann Ltd
Bullsbrook Road
Hayes, Middlesex, UB4 OJR
Tel: 0208 589 1600
UK email:
perivale@gueterman.com
Europe email:
mail@guetermann.com

John Lewis
Nationwide chain of
department stores
Tel: 0845 604 9049 for stores
and website ordering details

JosyRose Ltd
PO Box 44204
London, E3 3XB
Tel: 0207 537 7755
www.josyrose.com

Ribbonmoon
43 Banbury St
Talke
Stoke on Trent
Staffs, ST7 1JG
www.ribbonmoon.co.uk

U-Handbag
150 McLeod Road
London, SE2 OBS
Tel: 0208 310 3612
www.u-handbag.com

US

Bag Lady Press
PO Box 2409
Evergreen CO 80437-2409
Tel: (303) 670 2177
Email: baglady@baglady.com
www.baglady.com

Beadbox
1290 N. Scottsdale Road
Tempe Arizona 85281-1703
Tel: 1-800-232-3269
www.beadbox.com

Distinctive Fabric

2023 Bay Street

Los Angeles

CA 90021

Tel: 877 721 7269

www.distinctivefabric.com

Gütermann of America Inc

8227 Arrowbridge Blvd

PO Box 7387

Charlotte

NC 28241-7387

Tel: (704) 525 7068

Email: info@gutermann-us.com

J&O Fabrics

9401 Rt. 130

Pennsauken

NJ 08110

Tel: 856 663 2121

www.jandofabrics.com

Acknowledgments

Many thanks to Karl Adamson for trekking all the way up north to take the step photography, and to my lovely husband for putting up with me when the deadlines drew close!

About the author

Sally Southern is a textile artist and designer living and working in the seaside town of Cullercoats in the north east of England. She contributes regularly to craft magazines, is a community art worker, designs children's fashion and furnishing fabrics and produces her own work. She lives with her husband Stephen and young daughter Kitty, who, like her mum, has an unhealthy interest in all things sparkly, button-like and beaded!

Index